Following in part an old Indian trail through the wilderness, the National (or Cumberland) Road, begun under Jefferson in 1806, was the nation's first great highway, hailed in its day as "America's Appian Way." It was the only highway ever built directly by the federal government. It leaped the rugged Alleghenies to link the East Coast with the Mississippi Valley, and so was the road by which most of the pioneers went west. Presidents such as Andrew Jackson traveled it regularly, often stopping to shake hands with bystanders. In its heyday it was truly the national road, and the only highway in America ever to have that honor. It was eclipsed by the railroad and became a ghost road in the later nineteenth century, but it rumbled back to life with the coming of the automobile and lives on today as U.S. 40. Its story is told here by those who have known it best: those who have traveled it—from wilderness trail to modern highway—by foot, horseback, Conestoga wagon, packhorse, stagecoach, freight wagon, mail coach, hired hack, Model-T Ford, tractor-trailer truck, and modern automobile.

Traveling
The National Road

*Across the Centuries
on America's First Highway*

Traveling
The National Road

*Across the Centuries
on America's First Highway*

MERRITT IERLEY

THE OVERLOOK PRESS
Woodstock, New York

Frontispiece: Andrew Jackson at a stagecoach stop on the National Road

First published in 1990 by
The Overlook Press
Lewis Hollow Road
Woodstock, New York 12498

Copyright © 1990 by Merritt Ierley

Design: Abigail Sturges

Library of Congress Cataloging-in-Publication Data

Ierley, Merritt.
    Traveling the National Road : across the centuries on America's first highway / by Merritt Ierley.
    p.   cm.
    1.   Cumberland Road.   I.   Title.
  HE356.C8I37   1990
  388.1'22'0977—dc 20   89-77361   CIP
  ISBN 0-87951-394-2

2nd printing

Contents

Cumberland ("We live in a fast age") and then records his
impressions of the road

Acknowledgments

For their assistance in a variety of ways, my grateful acknowledgment to Gary J. Arnold, head of reference services, Ohio Historical Society, Columbus, Ohio; Michele Bottorff, director, Wayne County Historical Museum, Richmond, Indiana; David M. Buchanan, executive director, Historical Museum of the Wabash Valley, Terre Haute, Indiana; A. Vernon Davis, editor and publisher, *The Maryland Cracker Barrel,* Hagerstown, Maryland; John Frye, Washington County Public Library, Hagerstown, Maryland; Kathleen Knode, Williamsport Public Library, Williamsport, Maryland; David W. Kraeuter, College Historical Collection, Washington and Jefferson College Library, Washington, Pennsylvania; Dick Reynolds, retired managing editor, *The Palladium-Item,* Richmond, Indiana; Carney Rigg, National Park Service, Fort Necessity National Battlefield, Farmington, Pennsylvania (for her capable review of the manuscript); Martha Jordan Weygant, Burlington, Iowa (for permission to use excerpts from Philip Jordan's, *The National Road* [1948, Bobbs-Merrill Co.; copyright renewed, 1976, Philip Jordan]).

Photographs not otherwise credited are by Merritt Ierley, as is the map of the National Road.

"In the beginning, a thread of earth through dense and silent forest."
An overgrown remnant of the Braddock Road, predecessor of the
National Road, as photographed in 1949.

Courtesy of the National Park Service, Fort Necessity National Battlefield

Prologue

In the beginning, a primeval passage through the wilderness: the trampled trace of bison and other wild beast, rumbling from feeding ground to feeding ground, creating a strategic route through dense and silent forest.

Then trace turns to path: though still overrun with brush and but one traveler wide, a path stamped into the earth by countless step of moccasin-clad foot, the streams along its way often made passable by the placement of fallen trees. And then a trail: trader and explorer treading its way, cutting back the underbrush, their steps followed by those of columns of soldiers bound for the frontier, hacking away to make it wider and still more easily passable.

Free of the growth and brush that once owned it, a primitive road now: its earthen surface stamped with the hoofprints of horses, in pairs and then multiple pairs, framed by the ruts of wagon wheels—simple ox carts at first, then broad-wheeled Conestoga wagons in snowy caravans, then brightly painted stagecoaches with four or six proud horses galloping in front. The earthen surface gives way now to a primitive macadam, and the fallen trees to stately stone-arched bridges. What was once a path through the wilderness is now a mighty corridor—a grand highway, a National Road, from the mountains to the prairies.

But hush. Those pounding hoofs and screeching wheels are about to give way to a relative silence once again. It will be a quieter walk along this great avenue of history as, in the distance, we hear the sound of a new national road—the shrill whistle of a train. This new road will sweep up the traffic of America and hurl it westward, or otherward, at hitherto unknown speeds and comfort.

Yet wait: Americans are an independent and peripatetic people. Trains run at the mandate of schedules and routes; wagons and carriages—especially horseless wagons and carriages—run at the whim of people. A new sound now, not in the distance but on the old road itself—a klaxon horn, raucous as all get-out. Make a way, it seems to shout. Make a new highway out of the old road: paved, with modernized macadam here, and even concrete there.

Gone now the bumps and "thank-you-ma'ams" that sent heads into roofs of stagecoaches; gone the unguarded cliffs that coaxed wagons into oblivion; gone the snakelike curves of S-shaped bridges that, while perfectly suitable for coaches going 5 or 6 miles an hour, proved perfectly suicidal for cars reaching speeds of 50 or 60 miles an hour.

A modern highway: path and strategic route of the automobile.

But that's getting ahead of the story. Let's go back, now, to a primeval passage through the wilderness to begin our travels, guided by those who have gone this way before.

A National Road Gazetteer

A guide to sites and geographic features frequently mentioned in the text:

Baltimore-National Pike. The easternmost section of the National Road (Baltimore to Cumberland); conceived in 1797 when a group of Baltimore bankers and businessmen, seeking an increase in trade with the rapidly developing western territories, pledged joint resources to built a road west. From the start it produced profits from an increase in trade, plus as much as 20 percent a year in profit from the tolls collected. Though not technically a part of the National Road, popularly thought of as such by those who traveled it (see "National Road"); also known as National Pike and Baltimore Pike, and in sections as Bank Road, Frederick Pike, Boonsboro Pike and Frederick and Boonsboro Turnpike.

Big Crossings. See *Great Crossings*

Braddock's Road. Connected the Potomac River at Cumberland with the Monongahela River at Turtle Creek just south of what is now Pittsburgh; built by British Major General Edward Braddock in 1755 for his march on Fort Duquesne; followed route of Nemacolin's Trail, which was widened and extended; the basic route of the National Road through the Allegheny Mountains.

Casselman River. A tributary of the Youghiogheny River in southwestern Pennsylvania and northwestern Maryland; in old accounts, sometimes written "Castleman" or "Castleman's" River.

Cumberland Road. That portion of the National Road between Cumberland, Maryland, and Springfield, Ohio, officially designated "Cumberland Road" by Act of Congress. Legislation signed into law by Jefferson in 1806; construction was begun in 1811 but delayed in part by the War of 1812; completed to Wheeling (except for occasional unpaved sections) in 1818, and to Springfield in the mid-1830s.

Great Crossings. Also called Big Crossings, the crossing of the Youghiogheny River at what is now Youghiogheny River Lake, near Confluence, Pennsylvania. A modern bridge carries Route 40 traffic. The original National Road bridge remains, but under water; when the lake was created as a reservoir in 1944, the bridge disappeared some 50 feet below normal summer level of about 1,440 feet above sea level; lake is usually lowered in winter, but degree depends on summer rainfall, so that some winters, most of the bridge is visible, and others, none. See also *Somerfield.*

Great Meadows. Widest clear expanse in the Alleghenies, just south of U.S. 40 about 11 miles east of Uniontown, Pennsylvania; site of Fort Necessity; a mile west is the site of Braddock's Grave.

Gwinn's (or Gwynn's). A well-known tavern near the Six Mile Toll House, six miles west of Cumberland; sometimes called the "Six-Mile House." Established by Evan Gwinn while the road was still Braddock's Road; destroyed by fire about 1900.

Laurel Hill. The last great ridge of the Alleghenies going west, beyond which is Uniontown, Pennsylvania.

Little Crossings. The crossing of the Casselman River near Grantsville, Maryland; old bridge preserved as part of state park after being replaced in 1933 by a new bridge on a new right of way immediately adjacent to old road.

Little Meadows. A clear expanse on the west slope of Meadow Mountain, near Little Crossings, about 20 miles west of Cumberland; so called on the records of the Braddock expedition to indicate the site of the fourth encampment.

Madonna of the Trail. A series of twelve identical statues commemorating pioneer mothers of covered-wagon days, each a figure of a pioneer woman with two young children; in all National Road States except Maryland, the location is on National Road; erected in 1928 and 1929 by the National Society of the Daughters of the American Revolution. Located (east to west) in Bethesda, Maryland; Washington (Beallsville), Pennsylvania; Wheeling, West Virginia; Springfield, Ohio; Richmond, Indiana; Vandalia, Illinois; Lexington, Missouri; Council Grove, Kansas; Lamar, Colorado; Albuquerque, New Mexico; Springerville, Arizona; and Upland, California.

The Narrows. A gap nearly a mile long in Wills Mountain just northwest of Cumberland, Maryland, traversed by Wills Creek; often called the "Gateway to the West." The existing (1832) alignment of the National Road through The Narrows follows Wills Creek through this gap, whereas the original alignment (1806) followed the route of Braddock's Road over the mountain to the southwest; the new alignment was longer but considerably flatter, making it far preferable for the wagons and coaches that had become the major part of the road's traffic.

National Road. Strictly speaking, the road between Cumberland, Maryland, and Vandalia, Illinois, largely built by the federal government. The section between Baltimore and Cumberland, built through private initiative, is also frequently considered part of the National Road, though it is often referred to locally as the Baltimore-National Pike or National Pike. The National Road includes the Cumberland Road, the section between Cumberland and Springfield, Ohio; called National Road through common usage (only "Cumberland Road" was an official designation); west of the Ohio River, routed so as to connect capitals of the emerging states—Columbus, Ohio; Indianapolis, Indiana; and Vandalia, then the capital of Illinois. In this book, National Road is considered to mean the entire road of some 750 miles from Baltimore to Vandalia, just as it was known to mean to most travelers over the years.

National Pike or Turnpike. Another popular term for both the National Road and the Baltimore-National Pike.

Negro Mountain. One of the ridges of the Alleghenies in northwestern Maryland/southwestern Pennsylvania, west of Grantsville, Maryland; so called for an otherwise unknown black man of gigantic size who, with a volunteer company under Captain Thomas Cresap, helped defend white settlements against Indian attack and was killed in a skirmish on this mountain in 1754.

Nemacolin's Trail. The first established route from Cumberland west, marked out along existing Indian trails in 1751 by the Delaware Indian Nemacolin for Captain Thomas Cresap, an organizer of the Ohio Company. The path was "blazed" with ax marks on trees, a practice that became common among white men but was virtually never used by the Indians. The trail connected the Potomac River at Cumberland with the Ohio River near what is now Pittsburgh; most important early route to the Ohio Valley; basic route of Braddock's Road and, through the Alleghenies, of the National Road.

"Shades of Death." A dense forest of white pine east of Meadow Mountain, in Maryland, through which the National Road passed; so called because even the sunlight of a bright day was blocked out, making the forest perpetually dark and gloomy; this was a place feared by travelers, a logical hideout for hostile Indians and highway robbers. By the early 1900s, virtually the whole forest had been cut down, its wood used as pine shingles for new houses.

Smithfield. See *Somerfield.*

Somerfield. A largely extinct town in Pennsylvania on the Youghiogheny at Great Crossings; originally called Smithfield but renamed by the Post Office Department to avoid confusion with other places called Smith; effectively taken off the map in 1944, when the Youghiogheny was dammed to create a reservoir (Youghiogheny River Lake), inundating most of Somerfield. See also *Great Crossings.*

Tomlinson's. Perhaps the most famous tavern on the old road, also known as the Stone House or Stone House Inn and sometimes as Tumblestone's; on west slope of Meadow Mountain, just east of what is now U.S. 219. Established by Jesse Tomlinson on Braddock's Road near present site at least as early as 1775, when it was visited by Nicholas Cresswell, an English loyalist Indian trader (October 11, 1775: "lodged at Tumblestones on top of the Allegany Mountain"); visited by George Washington (who called it Tumberson's) in 1784; new tavern built close by on present site in 1815 during construction of National Road; James K. Polk dined here on the way to his inauguration in 1845. Now a private residence without even a plaque to commemorate its illustrious past.

Vandalia. Second state capital (1820–39) of Illinois.

Wills Creek. A tributary of the Potomac River, into which it flows at Cumberland, Maryland; until the winter of 1754–55, when Fort Cumberland was built, also the name of the settlement at this site.

Youghiogheny River (pronounced Yock-a-ganey). Rising near the West Virginia–Maryland border, it flows through Pennsylvania into the Monongahela River south of Pittsburgh; its spelling may be encountered in about as many variations as the number of letters in its name.

I. FROM A THREAD
OF EARTH

*A trail through the wilderness,
and its evolution to a road*

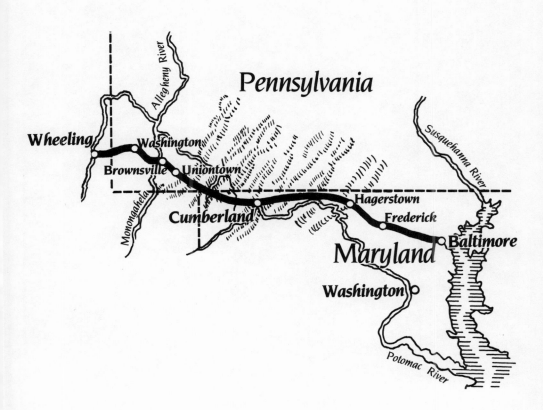

Trace turns to path with countless step of moccasin-clad foot, and then
to trail as soldier and settler make it theirs.

A THREAD OF EARTH

The first settlers arriving on the eastern shores of America must have thought the American continent an endless woodland, for what they found—nearly at the shoreline, except for occasional coastal marshes—were dense forests of pine, oak, spruce, and fir. So seemingly impenetrable were these woodlands that even the natives appeared to need canoes to go inland any distance.

What these early settlers, remaining on the coast, could not yet see was that the Indians traveled on land as well as water and had developed an extensive network of inland trails. Some were portage paths connecting major waterways; the Indian traveler, having reached the limit of navigation on one river, could easily haul his birchbark vessel on his back to another river and continue his journey. When settlers finally did venture inland— as traders, trappers, missionaries, mappers, adventurers, soldiers— they often found these paths ready-made for their own needs.

Many paths, including some of those for portage, predated even the American Indian. These were created in time immemorial by that original road builder, the wild beast, especially the buffalo, which once roamed as far east as central Pennsylvania. These buffalo paths were strategic passageways for migration or access to feeding grounds, and were, in the opinion of a traveler named John Bradbury, in 1810, "excellent roads." "I had frequent opportunities of examining [them]," he wrote, "and am of opinion that no engineer could have laid them out more judiciously."

The Indian, discovering this, made the same paths his own strategic routes for hunting, while also creating new pathways of his own—some to connect villages, others for making war on hostile tribes. Whatever the use, these were paths of the most primitive sort: always single-file; notably crooked, for the Indian would rather bypass an obstacle than remove it; and generally so overgrown with brush and trees that the traveler had to spread branches before him as he walked. The paths were unmarked, for it was the white man, not the Indian, who blazed trails by notching the bark of trees.

As settlers slowly began migrating westward (even at the beginning of the American Revolution, settlement generally extended only some 70 miles inland), and as trading increased, these Indian trails, time-proven, became the early roads of the white man. One such route had provided the Indians with portage from the headwaters of the Potomac River, at what is now Cumberland, Maryland, to the Monongahela River, south of the present Pittsburgh, by which the Ohio River, and hence all of the known West, was easily accessible—a route now of great strategic importance to the white man.

But as an Indian path, it typically had no marks of identification, and indeed was not so much one single path as several, alternate, parallel paths, often meandering one among another. With the formation of the Ohio Company, in 1749, a clearly marked route to the Ohio Valley had become essential. In 1751, two good friends—a founder of the Ohio Company by the name of Thomas Cresap (otherwise known as "Big Spoon," for his hospitality to friendly Indians) and a Delaware Indian named Nemacolin (who lived for some time with the Cresap family and whose son was eventually adopted by them)—collaborated to make this Indian trail a settler's trail, to make one easy-to-follow route out of a multiplicity of unmarked Indian paths. Westward from the Ohio Company's outpost at Wills Creek (the future Cumberland), axes in hand, they trod the slopes and slants of the rugged Alleghenies, notching tree after tree to show this most favorable route to the Monongahela River and the West. Known as Nemacolin's Trail, it was scarcely more than a thread of earth through the wilderness—yet a thread that could be followed.

*   *   *

Among the first to do so was a relatively little-known, twenty-one-year-old major named George Washington—the choice of Virginia Governor Dinwiddie in 1753 to carry, on behalf of the British government, an ultimatum to the French to depart the Ohio country. Though the mission was clearly a dangerous one, Washington perceived the honor of a signal service to colony and crown and was eager to take on the challenge, even knowing, from personal experience along the Virginia frontier, the adversity and danger that lay ahead, especially in winter.

Washington set out on horseback from Williamsburg October

31, 1753, with an interpreter and four retainers, adding guide Christopher Gist to the group along the way. Using in part Nemacolin's Trail, they traveled nearly to Lake Erie to find the French commandant, only to have him summarily reject the ultimatum. Washington recorded the entire trip in a journal; and in the form of a report to the governor, it was published the following year in Williamsburg, gaining wide notice both in America and England.

The excerpt included here is an exception for this book in that it transcends the route of the National Road, this account beginning at the Allegheny River, north of Nemacolin's Trail; from there, however, Washington follows that trail and finally the route of the future National Road into Wills Creek (Cumberland). The narrative keenly depicts the hardship of inland travel at that time and place and was the first published account of someone actually traveling along the future National Road. As this excerpt begins, Washington and Gist are returning home after presenting the ultimatum—alone and on foot, without tent or other supplies, their horses having given out. They are crossing the Allegheny River two miles east of Shannopin's Town (now Pittsburgh).

GEORGE WASHINGTON, 1753-54
On Foot, Allegheny River to Cumberland

Washington as a young officer.

[Saturday, December 29, 1753]
... We expected to have found the River frozen, but it was not, only about 50 Yards from each Shore: The Ice I suppose had broken up above, for it was driving in vast Quantities.

There was no Way for getting over but on a Raft: Which we set about [to make], with but one poor Hatchet, and finished just after Sun-setting. This was a whole Day's Work: we next got it launched, and went on Board of it: Then set-off. But before we were Half Way over, we were jammed in the Ice, in such a Manner that we expected every Moment our Raft to sink, and ourselves to perish. I put out my setting Pole to try to stop the Raft, that the Ice might pass by; when the Rapidity of the Stream threw it with so much Violence against the Pole, that it jirked me out into ten Feet Water: But I fortunately saved myself by catching hold of one of the Raft Logs. Notwithstanding all our Efforts we could not get the Raft to either Shore; but were obliged, as we were near an Island, to quit our Raft and make to it.

Washington and Gist crossing the Allegheny River in December 1753
—*"as fatiguing a Journey as it is possible to conceive."*

The Cold was so extremely severe, that Mr. Gist had all his Fingers, and some of his Toes frozen; and the Water was shut up so hard, that we found no Difficulty in getting off the island, on the Ice, in the Morning [Sunday, December 30], and went to Mr. Frazier's. We met here with 20 Warriors who were going to the Southward to War: But coming to a Place upon the Head of the great Kunnaway [Kanawha River], where they found seven People killed and scalped (all but one Woman with very light Hair) they turned about and ran back for Fear the Inhabitants should rise and take them as the Authors of the Murder. They report that the Bodies were lying about the House, and some of them much torn and eaten by Hogs: By the Marks which were left, they say they were French Indians of the Ottoway Nation, &c., who did it.

[Monday, December 31] As we intended to take Horses here, and it required some Time to find them, I went-up about three Miles to the Mouth of the Yaughyaughgane [Youghiogheny River] to visit [the Delaware Indian] Queen Alliquippa, who had expressed great Concern that we passed her in going to the Fort. I made her a Present of a Matchcoat and a Bottle of Rum; which latter was thought much the best Present of the two.

Tuesday the 1st Day of January [1754], we left Mr. Frazier's House, and arrived at Mr. Gist's at Monongahela the 2nd, where I bought a Horse, Saddle, &c. The 6th we met 17 Horses loaded with Materials and Stores for a Fort at the Forks of Ohio [Pittsburgh], and the Day after some Families going-out to settle: This Day [January 7, 1754] we arrived at Wills Creek [Cumberland], after as fatiguing a Journey as it is possible to conceive, rendered so by excessive bad Weather. From the first Day of December to the 15th, there was but one Day on which it did not rain or snow incessantly; and throughout the whole Journey we met with nothing but one continued Series of cold wet Weather, which occasioned very uncomfortable Lodgings; especially after we had quitted our Tent, which was some Screen from the Inclemency of it.

EVOLUTION TO A ROAD

The thread of earth that was Nemacolin's Trail was barely more than two feet wide in most places. It could hardly remain so thin a strand with the coming of the white man.

The evolution of this wilderness trail into a road, however, had much of its impetus far from the wilds, for it was in the courts of Europe that the future of the American continent was being determined. England (leagued with Prussia and Hanover) and France (with Austria, Russia, Saxony, Sweden, and Spain) had already fought three recent wars when Major George Washington was dispatched to warn the French back from the Ohio country, a warning rebuffed. Now the two major powers had become embroiled in a fourth and decisive war—the French and Indian—that would establish Britain's claim to North America.

The preliminary skirmish was fought along this evolving road. In the spring of 1754, Washington was again dispatched westward, as deputy commander of a Virginia detachment under Colonel Joshua Fry. After Fry died at Wills Creek on May 31, Washington took command. Even before, he had ordered an essential step in pressing Virginia's, and thus England's, claim to the Ohio Valley: widening Nemacolin's Trail so that his detachment of troops could more easily travel it, a job to which some sixty men were assigned. Their labors—now for a brief time called Washington's Road—improved the trail, yet Washington seriously considered giving up wagon travel for boats once he arrived at the Monongahela River. Before that would come to pass, he had reached Great Meadows, where he stood his ground against the French, at that hastily built fortification he himself named Fort Necessity; on the 4th of July, 1754, he would surrender it to the French.

What made this war different was that Britain chose to do its own fighting. Heretofore, Britain had considered the wars in America to be provincial affairs and had left most of the fighting to the American colonists. Now Britain was prepared to make its own significant commitment of both troops and leadership. Thus, in London, in September 1754, the Duke of Cumberland, captain-general of the entire British army and namesake of Fort Cumberland, summoned Major General Edward Braddock to be generalissimo of all his Britannic Majesty's troops on the American continent.

Braddock's first mission was to take Fort Duquesne from the French. For this, he had some 2,100 British regulars and Virginia militia, and as many Indians as he could recruit; but more important, he had the massive engines of war the provincials lacked, up to and including howitzers needing nine horses apiece to haul them.

A widened Indian trail would no longer do. Braddock set out to build a real road. Those road builders of old, bison and aborigine, were succeeded now by masses of soldiers. A company of 600 men set out from Fort Cumberland May 30, 1755, to clear the road west, hacking away with axes and saws, following closely Nemacolin's thread. Obstacles like huge trees, that the

Fort Cumberland in 1755.

Lowdermilk, *History of Cumberland*

"The Indians came, and an Interpreter was directed to tell them their Brothers, the English, were their friends, and every misunderstanding in past times should now be buried under that great Mountain, which was close by."—Orders for a Council of War at Fort Cumberland.

The Narrows, Cumberland, Maryland.

Indian snaked his trail around, fell to the woodsman's ax; overhanging brush was cut back; and the whole was now at last clearly marked—by its unmistakable presence in a pristine wilderness. This was Braddock's Road, twelve feet wide; and over it rumbled the phalanx of a new civilization that would eventually transform not only an Indian trail but an entire continent.

*   *   *

Among the marchers were two chroniclers of the Braddock expedition. Incongruous as it would first appear, one was a seaman—one of thirty on loan to Braddock from Commodore Augustus Keppel, commander of the British navy's North American Station at Hampton Roads. The seamen had a unique role with the expedition: to use their knowledge of ropes and rigging to get the heavily loaded military wagons, and especially the gun carriages, down the steep slopes of the Alleghenies. The horses had sufficient power for going uphill, but given the steepness of the mountains and the primitive nature of the road, wagon brakes were thought inadequate for going down. Hence the seamen to use block and tackle to control the rate of descent.

The name and rank of the writer of the account is unknown, though it is likely he was an officer. Although his journal is largely a record of the expedition itself, the excerpt here is about Fort Cumberland on the eve of march and the Indians of the region who were the original travelers of the trail.

Following the seaman's account is that of Captain Robert Orme, an officer in the Coldstream Guards on temporary assignment to General Braddock, whose journal is the most complete account of Braddock's expedition.

A SEAMAN WITH BRADDOCK'S ARMY, 1755
Cumberland

May 11th: Fort Cumberland is Situated within 200 Yards of Wills Creek on a Hill 400 Yards from the Potomack...it is built with Loggs drove into the Ground: and 12 feet above it Embrazures are cut for 12 Guns which are 4 Pounders, though 10 are only Mounted with loopholes for small Arms; The Indians were greatly surprised at the regular way of our Soldiers Marching and our Numbers.

I would willingly say something of the customs & manners of them, but they are hardly to be described. The Men are tall, well made and Active, but not strong; The Women not so tall yet well proportion'd & have many Children; they paint them-

A seaman of the
1700s/early 1800s.

selves in different Manners: Red, Yellow & Black intermixt, the
Men have the outer Rim of their Ears cut; and hanging by a
little bit at Top and bottom: they have also a Tuft of Hair left at
Top of their Heads, dress'd with Feathers... Their Match Coat
which is their chief Cloathing, is a thick Blanket thrown round
them; and instead of Shoes wear Mekosins, which laces round
the foot and Ankle... their manner of carrying Children are by
lacing them on a Board, and tying them with a broad Bandage
with a place to rest their feet, and Boards over their Heads to
keep the Sun off and this is Slung to the Womens backs.

May 12th: Orders for a Council of War at the Head Quarters
when the Indians came, and were received by the Guard with
Rested Arms, an Interpreter was directed to tell them that their
Brothers, the English, who were their friends were come to
assist them, that every misunderstanding in past times should
now be buried under that great Mountain (which was close by)
and Accordingly the Ceremony was perform'd in giving them a
string of Wampum or Beads...

May 13th: The Indian Camp were ¼ Miles from the Fort
which I went to visit their Houses are composed of 2 Stakes,
drove into the Ground, with a Ridge Pole & Bark of Trees laid
down the sides of it, wch. is all they have to Shelter them from
the Weather....

May 20th: Capt. Gates March'd into Camp with his New York Compy. The Indians met at the Generals Tent, and told him they were highly Obliged to the Great King their Father, for sending such Numbers of Men to fight for them, and they moreover promise to Join them, and do what was in their power by reconnoitring the Country, & bringing Intelligence ... Their Chiefs Names were as follows[:]

1st[:] Monicatoha [Monacatuca] their Mentor[;] 2d[:] Belt of Wampum, or white Thunder, who always keep the Wampum, and has a Daughter call'd bright Lightning[;] 3d: The great Tree and Silver Heels, Jimy Smith and Charles [called] all, belonging to the 6 Nations. The General Assured them of his Friendship and gave his Honour, that he never would deceive them, after which they sung their Song of War, put themselves into odd postures, wth Shouting and making an uncommon Noise, declaring the French to be their perpetual Enemies ... Arrived 80 Waggons from Pensylvania with Stores; and 11 likewise from Philidelpha with Liquors, Tea, Sugar, Coffe &c....100 Carpenters were Employed in making a Float, building a Magazine & squaring Timber to make a Bridge over Wills Creek, The Smiths were making Miners Tools, The Bakers were baking Biscuit, and every thing was getting ready for a March.

ROBERT ORME, 1755
On Horseback, Cumberland to near Uniontown

[June 7]
It appearing to the General [Braddock] absolutely necessary to leave some proper person to superintend the commissaries, and to dispatch the convoys, and also to command at the Fort, Colonel Innys was appointed Governor of it. Instructions were given to him, and money was left with him for contingent expenses, lest the service should for want of it meet with any checks.

Every thing being now settled, Sr Peter Halket with the 44th regiment marched the 7th of June.

Lieutenant Colonel Burton with the independent Companies and Rangers on the 8th, and Colonel Dunbar with the 48th regiment on the 10th, with the proportions of baggage, as was settled by the Council of War.

The same day the General left Fort Cumberland, and joined the whole at Spendlow camp, about five miles from the Fort [about halfway between Cumberland and Frostburg on the route of the National Road].

Robert Orme.

Pennsylvania Magazine of History, 1914.

June 11th. This day was employed in shifting the powder, fitting the waggons, and making a proper assortment of the stores.

The loads of all the waggons were to be reduced to fourteen hundred weight; seven of the most able horses were chose[n] for the Howitzers, and five to each twelve-pounder, and four to each waggon. The other horses were all to carry flour and bacon. Every horse was by contract to have carried two hundred weight, but the contractors were so well acquainted with our situation (which did not permit us to reject anything), that most of the horses furnished by them were the offcasts of Indian traders, and scarce able to stand up under one hundred weight.

It required two days to new load the waggons, and put everything in order, which being settled we marched on the 13th to Martin's plantation [just east of Frostburg], being about five miles from Spendlow Camp. The first brigade got to their ground that night, but the second could not get up before the next day at eleven of the clock, the road being excessively mountainous and rocky. This obliged the General to halt one day for the refreshment of men and horses.

June 15th. The line began to move from this place at five of the clock; it was twelve before all the carriages had got upon a hill which is about a quarter of a mile from the front of the Camp, and it was found necessary to make one-half of the men ground their arms and assist the carriages while the others remained advantageously posted for their security.

We this day passed the Aligany Mountain [Big Savage Mountain, following a course a mile or so north of the route of the National Road], which is a rocky ascent of more than two miles, in many places extremely steep; its descent is very rugged and almost perpendicular; in passing which we intirely demolished three waggons and shattered several. At the bottom of the mountain runs Savage river, which, when we passed was an insignificant stream; but the Indians assured us that in the winter it is very deep, broad and rapid. This is the last water that empties itself into the Potomack.

The first Brigade encamped about three miles to the westward of this river. Near this place was another steep ascent, which the waggons were six hours in passing.

In this day's march, though all possible care was taken, the line sometimes extended to a length of four or five miles.

June 16th. We marched from the Camp near Savage river to the little meadows [the west side of Meadow Mountain], which is about ten miles from Martin's Plantations, where the first brigade arrived that evening, but the second did not all arrive till the 18th. [This day's march included a region of dense pine forest known to later travelers as the "Shades of Death."]

By these four day's marches it was found impossible to proceed with such a number of carriages. The horses grew every day fainter, and many died; and the men would not have been able to have undergone the constant and necessary fatigue, by remaining so many hours under arms; and by the great extent of the baggage the line was extremely weakened.

The General was therefore determined to move forward with a detachment of the best men, and as little incumbrance as possible.

Therefore a detatchment of one field-officer with four hundred men and the deputy quarter master general marched on the 18th to cut and make the road to the little crossing ["Little Crossings"] of the Yoxhio Geni [actually the Casselman River, a fork of the Youghiogheny]—taking with them two sixpounders with their ammunition, three waggons of tools, and thirty five days provision—all on carrying horses. And on the 19th the General marched with a detachment of one Colonel, one Lieutenant Colonel, one Major, the two eldest Grenadier Companies, and five hundred rank and file.

The Indians were ordered to march with the advanced party; this day Monocatuca the Indian chief being at a small distance from the party was surrounded and taken by some French and Indians. The former were desirous of killing him, but the Indians refused, declaring they would abandon them and join with us if they persisted in their design. They agreed at last to tye him to a tree, and leave him: But his son who was with him escaped, and informed our Indians, who went soon after and brought him off.

We this day crossed the first branch of the Yoxio Geni, which is about four score yards over and knee deep. After having marched four miles from the little meadows we came up with the rear of the advanced party, and were obliged to encamp, as they were then at work in cutting a travers-road over an immense mountain [Negro Mountain], which could not be finished till the next day. Immediately upon coming to our ground, some guides ran into us, extremely frightened, and told us a great body of the enemy were marching to attack our advanced guard. The General sent forward an aid de camp to know the truth of this report, who found Lieutenant Colonel Gage in possession of the top of the mountain, and his men very advantageously posted. Our Indians had discovered the tracks of several men very near the advanced party, which had given rise to this alarm. Lieutenant Colonel Gage remained about two hours under arms, but no enemy appearing he sent parties to

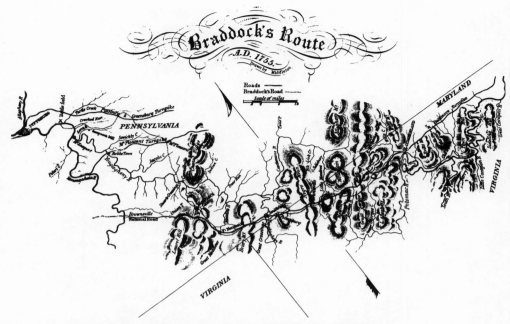

This map, published in 1855 on the 100th anniversary of Braddock's March, clearly shows the proximity of his route (dotted line) to the route of the future National Road (heavy line from Cumberland west). The two roads overlap in many places until diverging near Dunbar's Camp, where Braddock set his course for Fort Duquesne. What appears to be a heavy line east of Cumberland is the Potomac River.

scour the neighboring woods, and upon their return proceeded with the work, leaving proper parties to secure the heights, and encamped there that night.

June 19. From thence we marched about nine miles to Bear Camp [on the Maryland-Pennsylvania border] over a chain of very rocky mountains and difficult passes. We could not reach our ground 'till about 7 of the clock, which was three hours later than common, as there was no water, nor even earth enough to fix a tent, between the great Mountain and this place. We halted here two days.

On the 23rd of June we marched from this Camp to the Squaw's fort [on the east side of the Youghiogheny], making about six miles of very bad road.

The 24th of June we marched at five in the morning, and passed the second branch of the Yoxhio Geni [the Youghiogheny proper, at "Great Crossings"], which is about one hundred yards wide, about three feet deep, with a very strong current.

Braddock's March: Phalanx of a new civilization.

We marched this day about six miles, and at night joined the two detachments.

On the 25th, at daybreak, three men who went without the centinels, were shot and scalped. Parties were immediately sent out to scour the woods on all sides, and to drive in the stray horses.

This day we passed the Great Meadows, and encamped about two miles on the other side. We this day saw several Indians in the woods; the General sent the light horse, our Indians, and some volunteers, to endeavour to surround them, but they returned without seeing them.

About a quarter of a mile from this camp, we were obliged to let our carriages down a hill with tackles, which made it later than usual before we got to our ground.

Orders at the camp [included:] Every soldier or Indian shall receive five pounds for each Indian scalp.

June the 26th. We marched at five o'clock, but by the extreme badness of the road could make but four miles. At our halting place [Rock Fort Camp, on the east slope of Laurel Hill] we found another Indian camp, which they had abandoned at our approach, their fires being yet burning. They had marked in triumph upon trees, the scalps they had taken two days before, and a great many French had also written on them their names and many insolent expressions.

[At this point, near the present Mt. Summit, Pennsylvania, some ten miles southeast of Uniontown, the Braddock expedition turned north toward Fort Duquesne, leaving the general route of what would become the National Road.]

TYING WEST TO EAST

The French and Indian War over, Britain was left with huge war debts, which it sought in part to cover with increasingly oppressive taxes on the colonies; at the same time, it attempted to prevent another such war in the future through the simple expedient of preventing settlers from going west. By royal proclamation in 1763, George III prohibited settlement west of the Appalachian Mountains, an edict that undoubtedly had the deeper motive of preventing competition for Britain's lucrative fur trade. Enforcement in the great wilds of the known West, of course, proved impossible; and frontiersmen like Daniel Boone, in the Kentucky country of the early 1770s, pushed ahead anyway.

The early '70s was also a time of defiance in the East, as

*witness reaction to Britain's Tea Act of 1773. From Boston
Harbor the defiance radiated through the countryside—to
Lexington and Concord and then throughout the thirteen colonies. Defiance became war, and for the next seven years emigra-
tion to the west came to a virtual halt. The king, while losing his
colonies, at least found a way to enforce his edict of 1763.*

* * *

*The Revolutionary War over, an early pioneer of an overland
route west made a return visit to the Alleghenies, ostensibly to
inspect some land he now owned there but at least as much for
the purpose of encouraging travel between east and west.
George Washington, perhaps more than anyone at that time,
understood the need:*

> The Western Settlers—from my own observation—stand as it were on
> a pivet—the touch of a feather would almost incline them [either to
> England or to Spain].... The way to avoid both, happily for us, is
> easy, and dictated by our clearest interest. It is to open a wide door,
> and make a smooth way for the Produce of that Country to pass to
> our Markets.

*He saw it as America's destiny to have east and west firmly
linked. In Europe, a mountain chain so formidable as the
Alleghenies—nearly a hundred miles wide and a thousand miles
long, counting the whole of the Appalachian chain—would have
been thought a natural boundary intended by some intransmutable
law of nature to keep kingdoms separate. But as Washington
would have nothing to do with kingdoms in the New World,
neither would he accept as a national boundary a ridge of
mountains he himself could pass on foot in dead of winter.
There would have to be a road from east to west, and he had a
good idea of the most practical route.*

* * *

*Traveling on horseback with his nephew Bushrod, his old friend
Dr. James Craik, Craik's son, and several servants, Washington
left Mount Vernon September 1, 1784. This was a journey that
would take him 680 miles in five weeks, some of it over
territory familiar to the now retired general. Braddock's old
road was no longer howitzer-wide; it had had relatively little
use during the Revolutionary War and in the years after, and the
wilderness was slowly converting it back into a thread of earth.
Yet neither was it as primitive as on his first trip. There were
now taverns here and there, and other sites and landmarks that
were becoming familiar to travelers, many of which Washington
recorded in the little oblong notebook he had with him.*

GEORGE WASHINGTON, 1784
On Horseback, Cumberland to near Uniontown

[September 10th]
The Road from the Old Town [Oldtown, Maryland, southeast of Cumberland] to Fort Cumberland we found tolerably good, as it also was from the latter to Gwins, except the Mountain which was pretty long (tho' not steep) in the assent and discent: but from Gwins to Tumberson's [Tomlinson's Tavern at Little Meadows] it is intolerably bad—there being many steep pinches of the Mountain—deep & Miry places—and very stony ground to pass over. After leaving the Waters of Wills Creek which extends up the Mountain (Alligany) two or three Miles as the Road goes, we fell next on those of George's Creek which are small—after them, upon Savage River which are considerable: tho' from the present appearance of them, does not seem capable of Navigation.

11th
Set out at half after 5 o'clock from Tumbersons, & in about 1½ Miles came to what is called the little crossing of the Yohiogany—the road not bad—this is a pretty considerable water and, as it is said to have no fall in it, may, I conceive, be improved into a valuable navigation; and from every acct. I have yet been able to obtain, communicates nearest with the No. Branch of Potomack of any other. Breakfasted at one Mounts or Mountains, 11 Miles from Tumberson's; the Road being exceedingly bad, especially through what is called the Shades of death. Bated at the great crossing, which is a large Water, distant from Mounts[']s 9 Miles, and a better Road than between that and Tumbersons—Lodged at one Daughertys a Mile & half short of the Great Meadows—a tolerable good House—the road between the Crossing and Daughertys is in places, tolerable good, but upon the whole indifferent: distant from the crossing 12 Miles.

12th
Left Daughertys about 6 Oclock,—stopped awhile at the Great Meadows and viewed a tenement I have there [a landholding of 234½ acres, on either side of Braddock's Road including the site of Fort Necessity, near what is now Farmington, Pennsylvania], which appears to have been but little improved, tho capable of being turned to great advantage, as the whole of the ground called the Meadows may be reclaimed at an easy comparitive expence & is a very good stand for a Tavern—Much Hay may

be cut here When the ground is laid down in Grass & the upland, East of the Meadow, is good for grain.

Dined at Mr. Thomas Gists at the Foot of Laurel [Hill], distant from the Meadows 12 Miles, and arrived at Gilbert Simpsons' [on Braddock's Road, north of Uniontown] about 5 oclock 12 Miles further. Crossing the Mountains, I found tedious and fatieguing. from Fort Cumberland to Gwins took me one hour and Ten minutes riding—between Gwins & Tumbersons I was near 6 hours and used all the dispatch I could—between Tumbersons and Mount's I was full 4 hours—between Mounts and the crossing upwards of 3 hours—between the crossing and Daughertys 4 hours—between Daughertys and Gists 4¼. And between Gists and Simpsons upwards of 3 hours and in all parts of the Road that would admit it I endeavoured to ride my usual travelling gate of 5 Miles an hour.

ASSERTING UNITY WITH THE WEST

The wildness and remoteness of the frontier prevailed. Britain, having lost its thirteen colonies, remained a presence in the back country, stirring up Indians against the pioneers and continuing to monopolize the fur trade. Even U.S. citizens, with passions as primitive as the land, were showing the very sort of independence that Washington had warned about. Their independence came to a head with the Whiskey Rebellion.

In 1791, the new federal government passed its first excise law, which included a tax on whiskey. It was a sharp blow to the farmers of western Pennsylvania, who had turned to wide-scale whiskey production for a simple reason: They had a surplus of grain, and the cost of transporting grain—especially in the absence of good roads across the Alleghenies—was greater than the cost of transporting whiskey. A wagon that could haul a ton of corn (or 36 bushels) at $1 per bushel, made $36 on arrival in Philadelphia; loaded instead with a ton of corn whiskey (or 220 gallons) at $1 per gallon, the same wagon could make $220.

Whiskey quickly became the basis of the region's economy. The new tax was thus a heavy blow, and many distillers turned to bootlegging rather than pay the tax. Federal agents cracked down and forced those who were caught to go to New York or Philadelphia for trial. Angry farmers responded by attacking a federal agent serving a process, destroying the home of the general in charge of excise enforcement, burning the barns of

The Whiskey Rebellion: Tarring and feathering an excise officer.

informers, and terrorizing court officials. Pittsburgh was threatened with armed attack.

For the new federal government, it was the first internal test of authority. President Washington, at the behest of Secretary of the Treasury Alexander Hamilton, called up the militia. Some 15,000 strong, they gathered in Virginia, Maryland, eastern Pennsylvania, and New Jersey and trooped westward to Pittsburgh in answer to their country's call. Against so great a show of force, hopelessly outnumbered protesters dispersed so quickly the militia had to comb the countryside looking for them. Only two were prosecuted, and both were later pardoned.

The Whiskey Rebellion affirmed the federal character of the new government and its authority to intercede locally. A few years later, a still broadening conception of federal authority would be expressed in the building of a national road simply because it served a national purpose—a road that would help keep in check this potentially troublesome frontier as well as provide for more efficient transportation of goods to market.

*   *   *

Among those who marched with the militia was Dr. Robert Wellford, an English-born surgeon who came to America with Britain's General Howe in 1775 and later defected to the American cause. As a surgeon with the Virginia militia, Wellford was among those called up to help suppress the Whiskey Rebellion. He kept a detailed journal of the march, which, between Fort Cumberland and Brownsville, traversed the route of the soon-to-be National Road.

ROBERT WELLFORD, 1794
On Horseback, Cumberland to Brownsville

Thursday, [October] 9th
... took up our quarters at Capt. Bells, at Fort Cumberland, 14 miles, making a journey of Sixty nine miles from Winchester.

10th
Attended to my professional duties, & dined this day with the Commander in Chief [Light-Horse Harry Lee of Revolutionary War fame, father of Robert E. Lee], in company with a number of Officers. Find ourselves comfortably quartered at Capt. Bells, as also the men, who are well encamped at the back of the Garden under the Marque & two Tents.

Saturday. 11th Oct'r.
All leisure time of the evening of yesterday & of this morning
has been occupied in writing to Mrs. W., &c., &c.

16th, Thursday.
Between eleven & twelve o'clock this day arrived the President
of the United States [Washington, who had considered advancing with the troops to Pittsburgh but, after conferring, returned
to Philadelphia for the opening of Congress November 3]
escorted into the town & to Head Quarters near the Fort by
three troops of light dragoons, every man of whom cheerfully
left the encampment to pay the President a compliment, every
regiment was drawn up in excellent order to receive him, & as
he passed the line of Infantry he deliberately bowed to every
officer individually. The Artillery at the same time announced
his arrival.

17th.
Was this day invited to dine with the President, and with a
number of officers, dined under Genl. Lee's Marque, and was
treated very affably by the President, who was pleased to
express his approbation of my conduct.

This morning the President of the United States set out for
Bedford [Pennsylvania, the rendezvous point for the militia] on
his return to the right wing of the Army, & from there to the
seat of Government.

Thursday, 23rd of Octr.
The left wing of the Army, with the Commander in Chief,
marched from Fort Cumberland to Strickers, 11 miles, & encamped
in a meadow.

24th.
From Strickers the Army proceeded this day to Tomlinson's, at
the little Meadows, 11 miles. The course of this day's march led
the Army over a thousand times ten thousand rocks, thro' a
dark, dreary part of the Mountains called the "Shades of Death,"
& by an almost continued ascent to that rugged and elevated
part of the Allegheny Mountains known by the epithet of the
"back bone of America." Towards evening it began to rain, and
the Tents of the Cavalry were pitched in the right hand meadow
directly opposite the former encampment of General Braddock,
and the ground on which Washington made a stand [actually at
Great Meadows] after Braddock's defeat, the marks of which are
now easily discernable. The Infantry & the Artillery fixed their
temporary residence in the edge of the woods above the little

meadows, which are in the State of Maryland. The rain increased during the evening, & the whole of the night.

26th.

Rained the whole of the last Night & looks very much like continuing as long as we remain here upon this spot, as we can occasionally see the clouds much lower than the ground we have lately passed.... It can then be readily conceived that clouds passing over the mountains would, from the interference of these mountain heights, cause the contents of the clouds to be prematurely showered down. Notwithstanding the rain, Genl. Orders were issued for the troops to march, & at 10 o'clock the tents were struck, & the Infantry & artillery proceeded to Simkins's, & the Cavalry as far as Mountains & Augustines. The distance from Tomlinson's at the little Meadows to the little crossing of Youghogany River, 3 miles, from the little crossings to Simkins, where the Commander in Chief made his Head Quarters, 8 miles, & from thence to Mountain's hovel & Augustine's hog stye, making a progress of 18 miles this day, altho' the rain never remitted until evening. This part of the world, & its inhabitants appeared to me to be in strict alliance with every thing that can be called filthy & undesirable.

27th, Monday.

Remained in this most uncomfortable situation the greater part of the day, a portion of which was by all the officers in the neighborhood devoted to visiting each other, without discovering anything that could lead to a wish for an exchange of Quarters. In the evening we made a party, and rode to Jone's, about two miles, were kept warm by a large fire, & had a more plentiful supper, & more whiskey produced for our use than we had since we left Fort Cumberland. This evening it again rained, which, if possible, increased our dissatisfaction.

Tuesday, the 28th of October.

Left this detestable part of America, & proceeded to the great crossings of the Youngogany (three miles) [across the Pennsylvania line], which, from the rapidity & depth of the water, was with some difficulty, & in several instances, with some danger forded by the Cavalry. A large boat & other vessels were provided for the passage of Foot Soldiers, &c.

Thursday, 30th of October.

At noon this day passed over the Laurel Hill & was witness to one of the most extensive & interesting views that the imagination can form. On the summit of a mountain of immense height you see in your rear a country composed of mountainous & rugged aspect as far as the eye can command, & of such appearance as to seem absolutely impassable if we were not satisfied that the contrary was a fact. To the right and left appear a most unfertile chain of rocky mountains. But in front you behold a vale beautiful indeed. At this season a most lovely verdure was retained, & the friendliness of the soil in promoting the growth of grass was evident upon every Farm, which every moment opened to view, & presented a most desirable prospect of near thirty well cultivated Estates & a small Town called Beesom Town alias Union Town. Into this Town, 12 miles from Bells, we entered about dining time, and my attention was immediately arrested by small water courses, which intersected the Town, & which indubitably contributed to the fine green colour of the paddocks & produce of the adjoining meadows. Dined at Collins Tavern with Major Lewis, & engaged with him a room, &c., at Mr. Kings.

Octr 31st.
The weather very bad. Nov'r 1st, 2nd, 3rd & 4th almost a constant rain the streets unaccountably mirey, which hourly exposed my health to all the bad consequences of feet constantly damp, & my situation requiring some share of activity, I was almost hourly exposed to every influential effect of Rain upon the human frame.

Novr 5th.
The Commander in Chief left this dirty place for Brownsville (alias Red-Stone), & all the troops (excepting the Guards for Hospital, &c.) marched out of Town in three divisions as expressed in the Genl Orders of the day. Early in the afternoon Mr. Glassell & Dr. Kerr arrived, & having established the hospital to the best of my ability, I left Dr. Kerr, Rawlings & Bennet entrusted with sick to the number of 116, & also Medical & Hospital stores, including a quarter Cask of Wine, &c. Then Mr. Glassell accompanied me to Brownsville, where I reported to Genl Lee the effective steps I had adopted for the relief and comfort of the unfortunate.

II. COMES A ROAD

The federal government, overcoming
political and Constitutional hurdles, steps in and
builds a road from East to West

Albert Gallatin

New York Public Library Picture Collection

THE FEDERAL GOVERNMENT STEPS IN

When the First Congress convened for the first time on March 4, 1789, there was no session because there was no quorum. Only nine senators and thirteen representatives were there to answer the roll call. The House did not have a quorum present until April 1; the Senate not until April 6. In large part this was due to bad weather in the south and west, and the fact that three states were still voting; but in part it owed to the primitiveness of the roads, which compounded the effects of the weather.

Roads at the beginning of the new republic were in the same condition as in colonial days—generally so poor that traveling conditions *improved* with a snowstorm: it was easier and more comfortable driving a sleigh over newly fallen snow than a carriage over a bare road in its usually deplorable condition. Even on the most important roads, stagecoach passengers were often compelled to get out and help the driver pull the vehicle from the mud. It was not uncommon to see horses in mud up to their haunches. Sticks or rails were often stuck into the road to warn travelers of mudholes or quicksand. Fences were sometimes pulled down so vehicles could bypass the road in favor of adjacent fields. One stretch of road in Maryland, between Elkton and the Susquehanna River, was so uneven and rutted that stagecoach passengers frequently were asked by the drive to lean out the side of the coach to prevent its overturning. "Now, gentlemen," he would say, "to the right"; "now, gentlemen, to the left."

As in England, roads were the responsibility of local authorities, and as from the time of the Middle Ages, they were

The Baltimore Pike, Baltimore, looking eastward from Waverly Terrace, ca. 1860.

The Baltimore National Pike (U.S. 40) at Carey Street, Baltimore—roughly the same location today.

maintained by the men of the community, who were required to work on the roads a number of days each year—or pay a highway tax to discharge their obligation.

Most commercial traffic in colonial times was waterborne along the coast. Packhorse trains were used for overland travel, where roads were nonexistent or too poor to be used by wagons. Yet the need for eventual development of roads was being recognized. Early in the 1700s, regular wagon freight service was established by government franchise between Perth Amboy and Burlington, New Jersey, effectively linking New York and Philadelphia. Throughout the century, commercial travel by cart and wagon increased—markedly so late in the 1700s. Boston between 1768 and 1798 recorded a 650 percent increase in the number of carts and wagons its residents owned—from 22 to 145; during roughly the same period Philadelphia experienced an even larger increase.

With the growing numbers of coaches and carriages as well as commercial vehicles came a growing demand for more adequate roads. In partial answer came the turnpike. The states of Virginia, Maryland, and Connecticut in the 1780s began charging tolls on certain of their roads in order to finance improvements. But the real toll roads were the turnpikes financed through private capital under government charter. The first was the Philadelphia and Lancaster Turnpike, chartered by Pennsylvania in 1792. Built in two years over a distance of 62 miles, it had a 24-foot-wide roadbed of crushed stone plus 6 feet of clearing on each side. Other turnpikes followed. A company financed largely by Baltimore merchants in 1797 began construction of a turnpike from Baltimore to Frederick. The Frederick Turnpike, as it was then called, was the first leg of what would become known as the Baltimore National Pike. Pennsylvania eventually chartered more than eighty turnpike companies, with a combined total of 2,400 miles, by the 1830s. New York by the 1820s had 278 companies, with more than 4,000 miles. Virginia in 1816 set up a board of public works to supervise turnpike construction. The states generally regulated turnpikes closely, setting both tolls and standards of construction.

By the 1840s, the popular type of pike was the plank road— one made of wood planks set side by side. Such a road was cheap to build and relatively smooth to ride on, but the planks had a short life span, and unless they were replaced frequently, they deteriorated into a surface not much better than the rutted road of old. The plank road was gradually abandoned. The turnpike itself, no match for the railroad or even the canal, eventually ran its course; and in time nearly all roads reverted to public maintenance with "forced labor"—if maintained at all.

As they were becoming popular, these pikes that were being built through private capital had two qualities in common: they were in, or connected to, population areas of sufficient density to make probable a good return on investment; and they were relatively easy to construct, so far as terrain was concerned. Neither was the case with a route across the sparsely populated, ruggedly mountainous Alleghenies. And yet the need for such a road there—a road and not merely a widened Indian trail—was even more clear by the beginning of the nineteenth century.

Let us turn now to a Swiss immigrant who arrived in America in 1780, thence to become an emigrant—as the early pioneer was known—and settle in the western Pennsylvania mountains in the neighborhood of the future National Road. A decidedly atypical backwoodsman, he was: a native of Geneva, of aristocratic birth; the scion of a family that, since the fourteenth century, had begotten his native city-state a succession of councilors, chief magistrates, clerics, professors, physicians, and military officers; a product of the Enlightenment, and a man of refinement and manners; and briefly an adjunct instructor in French at Harvard. His background notwithstanding, he found himself in 1784 in the wilds of the Alleghenies, taking up residence on the Monongahela River in what is now known as New Geneva, Pennsylvania, about 12 miles southwest of Uniontown.

The reason for this transplantation is that Albert Gallatin, a month short of his nineteenth birthday, renounced his family's intention to have him become a lieutenant colonel with the Hessian troops going to America on behalf of George III. He left Geneva to make a new life of his own in the "land of opportunity." He spent several years in New England, then struck up an acquaintance with a Frenchman, M. Savary, who had warrants for land in the Ohio Valley. Gallatin journeyed with Savary as far as western Pennsylvania; finding the land suitable there, he chose to sink his modest fortune in real estate.

Yet so erudite a man would hardly seem to be content living for long in the confines of his backwoods investment, and so with Gallatin. He entered state politics, becoming a member of the legislature in 1790. He played a key role in defusing the Whiskey Rebellion of 1794. Later that year he was elected to Congress, where he served until 1801. His forte quickly became finance, a result of which was his fathering of what is now the House Ways and Means Committee. So highly regarded was he for his eminence in finance, and so close an ally of Jefferson had he become, that he was the inevitable choice for secretary of the treasury with Jefferson's election as president. He served until 1814.

As the nation's chief fiscal executive, Gallatin personified both the Calvinism of Geneva and the pragmatism of his new homeland on the frontier. Gallatin's first priority was to pay off the public debt and balance the federal budget; that done, he would have the nation devote its financial resources to "cementing the bonds of the Union between those parts of the United States, whose local interests have been considered as most dissimilar." And the way to do that, as he personally knew: a vast federal building program of roads, canals, and other improvements. But in particular: a federally funded road from the eastern seaboard through Ohio, which was then seeking statehood.

Jefferson shared the dream, but believed the federal government lacked authority for internal improvements of so general a nature (the Constitution gave power only to "establish," not necessarily build, "post-offices and post-roads"); a Constitutional amendment would be necessary, he believed. Others in Congress thought that even with the authority of an amendment, the federal government ought not to be doing what the states could do for themselves.

Fundamental, however, was cost. Here Gallatin had an answer that appears to have made moot the question of authority. Writing in February 1802 to Representative William B. Giles, chairman of the House committee with jurisdiction over the statehood legislation, Gallatin proposed that "one-tenth part of the net proceeds of the [federal] lands hereafter sold by Congress shall . . . be applied towards laying out and making turnpike or other roads, first from [the Potomac River] to the Ohio, and afterwards continued through the new State; such roads to be laid out under the authority of Congress." Although Gallatin did not mention it by name, it is clear what he had in mind, for on his copy of the letter he later penned, "Origin of National Road." Since it was feared the new state might sell off unpaid-for government land for taxes, Congress agreed, but changed the amount to 5 percent—in retrospect no insignificant sum, since sales of land over the next thirty-five years came to nearly $20 million.

Even though it was later made 2 percent, that was enough. With this modest yet unprecedented funding, Congress in 1806 passed the legislation launching the National Road—for now officially designated the Cumberland Road. The legislation provided for a three-man Cumberland Road Commission to oversee construction and maintenance; it also set forth such specifications as width (4 rods, or 66 feet, cleared width, not paved, but a new standard nonetheless) and maximum grade (five degrees, or 8.75 percent, a remarkable requirement for such mountainous terrain). The route would be up to the president, based on the recommendations of the three commissioners, though a Senate committee headed by Uriah Tracy of Connecticut urged a route westward from Cumberland through Brownsville, Pennsylvania, reaching the Ohio River at some point between Wheeling and Steubenville, Ohio—the approximate route eventually selected and one that followed the course of Braddock's Road through the steeps of the Alleghenies.

Those broad outlines left vast work to be done in determining the actual route, work that could only be done out there in the wilds by the commissioners and their surveyors and mappers. Within months, Jefferson had named his commissioners, and they were on their way west. A national road that private capital had no interest in—because of both the sparsity of population and great difficulty of construction—was becoming a reality.

* * *

In the summer of 1806, Jefferson appointed Thomas Moore and Elie Williams of Maryland and Joseph Kerr of Ohio as commissioners of the Cumberland Road. As with other federal appointments then and since, the chief executive had no personal acquaintance with the appointee and relied on the judgment of an associate. In the case of Williams, Jefferson clearly had misgivings. As he wrote to Gallatin in August 1806: "Mr. R.S. has had a commission given to Eli Williams as commissioner of the Western road. I am sorry he has gone out of Baltimore for the appointment, and also out of the ranks of Republicanism. It will furnish a new matter for clamor."

In retrospect, Elie Williams (his name is often found as "Eli" but he used "Elie") performed with distinction and came to be highly regarded for the obvious zeal he brought to the task of laying out the National Road. And instead of furnishing a clamor, he furnished a handwritten journal of the commissioner's survey of the route of the new road.

He and the other two commissioners met in Cumberland September 3, 1806, to embark on their tour, but Williams's journal does not record its first entry until September 22, by which time the expedition—including two surveyors, two chain carriers, a vane man, a packhorse man, and a horse—had reached the Youghiogheny River, just north of the Pennsylvania border.

Bowing to the severity of the weather, the commissioners concluded their work the first week of December. The work was also hampered—as the commissioners noted in their report to President Jefferson December 30, 1806—by existing maps "not sufficiently accurate" and by "the solicitude and importunities of the inhabitants of every part of the district, who *severally conceived their grounds entitled to a preference" in determining the route of the road.*

Williams's journal is more prosaic than other early accounts but clearly one of great significance to the evolution of the National Road.

ELIE WILLIAMS, 1806
By Foot and Pack Horse, Youghiogheny River to Cumberland

Elie Williams. This oil portrait, a copy of a painting by Charles Willson Peale, hangs in the reading room of the Williamsport, Maryland, Memorial Library.

[Having surveyed as far west as Wheeling, Williams and his fellow commissioners are returning to Cumberland and have just crossed the Youghiogheny River in Pennsylvania. The route being surveyed in this narrative closely follows the old Braddock Road.]

Wednesday 26 Nov. Snowed till 11 oclock, the Commsrs then set out [into Maryland] with Mr. Simkins [presumably of Simkins's, an inn on Chestnut Ridge] examining the grounds along & near Braddock's road, found them capable of much improvement, the Negroe mountain may be crossed on grounds within the limits of the law [no grade to exceed five degrees] but not shorter than the present road, the Big Shade hill & little Yough hill may also be passed the same way without increase of distance, as may the other ground to Tomlinson's, here we lodged.

Thursday 27. The Commsrs accompanied by Jessee Tomlinson & Wm. Thistle [owner of another nearby inn] viewed grounds which improve the present road, leaving it on the left at the East end of Tomlinsons lane to raise the Meadow mountain at five degrees[,] cross the road on the eastside near the top, slope down it North Eastward by crossing little shade run North of the road and up a hollow in a direction towards Cranberry Spring with which these grounds may be connected, we then filed off at right angles to view a route marked by Anderson & others from a point at a marked tree near a mile south west of Haversticks, in tracing this route we found it bearing too much south for a direct route, passing Savage river without much difficulty & ascending that mountain in a south east direction to the top and across it down a spur of the mountain to Winebrenners [near Frostburg] this Spur we found descend too rapidly, but supposed another Spur a little more south by Barretts' old place would answer. Having on our way out viewed the grounds thus far from Cumberland we closed for the present the business of exploring and proceeded to Cumberland, where we lodged.

From Fryday 28th November till Saturday the 6th December inclusive the Commsrs were engaged at Cumberland in comparing their several journals of their proceedings in exploring & examining the grounds from the commencement and in making a decision on the grand points to be located for the direction of the route and after mature deliberation determined that the route commence at a stone at the corner of lot no. 1 in Cumberland & near the confluence of Wills Creek & the North Branch of Potomac, to extend thro the street westwardly to cross the hill laying between Cumberland & Gwynns [tavern] at the gap in said hill where Braddocks road passes...

Before the Commsrs came to this decision an unusual fall of snow at so early a period of the winter made it impossible for them to proceed in regulating & marking the route, they therefore concluded to relinquish further progress in the business till such a period in the Spring as the weather will permit them to resume and in the meantime to report to the President the progress made, and after instructing Mr. Thompson their Surveyor to prepare with all convenient dispatch a compleat & comprehensive map of all their work they left Cumberland under an engagement to meet at the City of Washington as soon as their journal & report could be made up to be presented with their plat to the President of the United States at the City of Washington.

BUILDING THE ROAD

In their report to President Jefferson in December 1806, Elie Williams and his fellow Cumberland Road commissioners observed that the task of surveying a route for the road had become "a work of greater magnitude, and a task much more arduous, than was conceived before entering upon it."

No less might have been said for building it. Both the geographic and political terrain were precipitous. As for the section of the Alleghenies the road would cross, a profile is possible using the commissioners' own calculations of elevation based on Cumberland (actually 688 feet above sea level) as ground zero. The road would begin at Cumberland (0), then have to rise to 2,022 at Savage Mountain, fall to 1,741 at the Savage River, rise to 2,026 at Meadow Mountain, fall to 1,322 at the Casselman River, rise to 2,328 at Negro Mountain, fall to 645 at the Youghiogheny River, rise to 1,550 at Laurel Hill, and fall to 274 at Uniontown—all within a span of 50 miles.

A surveyor, such as might have accompanied Elie Williams and the other commissioners.

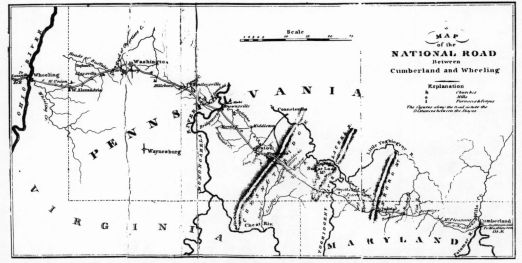

The National Road between Cumberland and Wheeling as constructed 1811–18.

J. Melish, *A Geographical Description of the United States,* 1826

To cross such terrain was a challenge enough; but the legislation creating the Cumberland Road also directed that the road be laid out so there was no grade in excess of 5 degrees—a remarkable standard for the time in so mountainous a country. Five degrees equals 8.75 percent, the latter being the form of measurement highway engineers now use. The Interstate Highway Act, in the age of bulldozers and dynamite, allows grades of up to 7 percent in rugged terrain. So the National Road in still another respect was an engineering marvel. A survey in 1818 of the just completed road between Cumberland and Uniontown, the most mountainous stretch, disclosed only one short ascent that failed to meet the standard (it was 5°15', "Notes of a Survey... October, 1818," National Archives).

How this was managed to so remarkable an extent was explained by the commissioners:

> "The face of the country within the limits prescribed is generally very uneven, and in many places broken by a succession of high mountains and deep hollows, too formidable to be reduced within five degrees of the horizon [except] by crossing them obliquely, a mode which, although it imposes a heavy task of hill-side digging, obviates generally the necessity of reducing hills and filling hollows, which, on these grounds, would be an attempt truly Quixotic."

In other words, by bending the requirement for being the straightest, the builders might satisfy the need to be the least steep; hence they compromised by winding the road through

Road building in the early 1800s. Most of the construction workers were Irish or English immigrants.

Cross section of the National Road. The lower layer was stone broken to pass through a seven-inch ring; the upper layer, a three-inch ring. The surface was of sand or gravel compressed with a three-ton roller. After the road was macadamized, the structure consisted of three layers of finer stone.

Road building in the early 1900s: work on the National Road west of
Frostburg, Maryland.

gentle horseshoe curves where the mountain was the steepest; then, where grade was not a factor, letting it fly as straight as an arrow.

Bending the rule about being the straightest route also helped to satisfy political considerations, and particularly "the solicitude and importunities" of each town and region as to the route. The 1806 report set a general route roughly following Braddock's Road, including as reference points such increasingly familiar landmarks as Tomlinson's tavern; but it bypassed such increasingly important towns as Uniontown and Washington, Pennsylvania.

As of early 1807, Pennsylvania had not given its approval to the Cumberland Road, and approval of the affected states was a prerequisite of the federal legislation. With Maryland and Virginia already on record as favorable, that meant Pennsylvania's approval was essential. It came in April 1807, but with a condition: the route recommended by the commissioners had to be changed to include both Uniontown and Washington. Even so, the commissioners continued plotting the route as originally planned. In July 1808, it was the towns' former representative in Congress—Albert Gallatin himself—who laid it on the line to Jefferson: "It was my impression that you had acquiesced, and would instruct the commissioners to [include Uniontown and Washington]. I find, however, that it has not been done, and I seriously fear the consequences at this time.... Permit me to state that the county of Washington ... gives a uniform majority of about 2000 votes in our favor, and that if this be thrown, by reason of this road, in a wrong scale, we will infallibly lose the State of Pennsylvania in the next election." Uniontown and Washington were duly added to the Cumberland Road.

With a route surveyed, and approved by the president in 1808, it probably seemed to many that a road ought to follow in short order. It did not. By the end of 1808, contracts had been let for clearing some of the right of way, and surveying was completed to Wheeling, but it was not until April 1811 that contracts were let for construction of the first 10 miles west of Cumberland—a section completed in September. Meanwhile, consensus had been reached on extending the road west of Wheeling, this portion by law to include the capitals of Ohio (Columbus), Indiana (Indianapolis), and Illinois (Vandalia). The road now also had a superintendent, David Shriver, Jr., to supervise construction and, as section by section was completed, oversee operation.

In September 1811, the first section was finished, and contracts were awarded for the second section of 11 miles. By the

Road building today: construction of an overpass on Rt. 40–48, the
National Pike, just east of Cumberland, Maryland.

"Masterly Workmanship...positively a Superb Bridge."—Uria Brown

The Casselman River Bridge near Grantsville, Maryland, built in 1813, as it appeared in the early days of motoring. Its 80-foot span was the largest stone arch in America at the time it was built.

The bridge today: no longer in use but open to tourists. It was replaced by a new bridge in 1933.

end of 1813, some 21 miles had been completed and work was starting on the next 20. The first of the National Road's many "noble arches of stone" was also complete: the Casselman River bridge, an 80-foot span that was the largest stone arch in America at the time. Indeed, many people wondered if it would stand. According to local tradition, the contractor, not wanting to take a chance, had his men remove the framework the night before as a test, and then replace it before the formal opening the next day. The bridge stood, and stands today.

As soon as a section of new road was finished, the public poured out upon it, often creating mass confusion as wagons and carriages quickly caught up with and mixed in with construction crews trying to get the next section finished. Yet, mile by mile, the road went on: hills leveled, huge stones hauled away, trees toppled, underbrush cut back, stumps pulled, roots grubbed out, the road itself then constructed in a clearing 66-feet wide. Ditches were dug at either side, leaving a sloped "cradle" 32-feet wide in the center; a section 20-feet wide was then dug out to a depth of 18 inches at the center and 12 inches at the sides and "metalled," or filled first with hand-crushed 7-inch stone, then by 3-inch stone, then by a surface of sand or gravel compressed by a 3-ton roller. A roadway.

For those living along the way, it was a not-to-be-forgotten sight: "a thousand strong" they came, wrote a farmer near Uniontown, "with their carts, wheel-barrows, picks, shovels, and blasting tools, grading those commons, and climbing the mountainside, leaving behind them a roadway good enough for an emperor to travel over."

Finally in 1818, except for a few sections still unpaved, the National Road was complete to Wheeling, and the first mail coaches began rumbling west from Washington, D.C. The road vibrated now to the beat of hoof and screech of iron wheel as countless travelers crossed it in a seemingly endless parade of wagons, carriages, ox carts, and conveyances of every description.

*   *   *

The first traveler to leave us a record of this one-time thread of earth as the National Road was Uria Brown in 1816. A Baltimore surveyor and conveyancer, he was also a devout Quaker. His journal is full of both the detail a surveyor might find of interest and also those broad and deeply religious perspectives that owe to his Quaker background. Others following in his steps and leaving us a record of their travels were Adlard Welby, an English gentleman visiting in America, and James Hall, twenty-six, a native of Philadelphia and future author, on his way to the Ohio Valley to make his home.

URIA BROWN, 1816
On Horseback, Cumberland to Brownsville

[Wednesday, June 19]
Called my [lodging] bill & paid the same—$1.91. Thence from
Old Town 15 Miles...to Cumberland, formerly Fort Cumberland.
I arrived here about 3 o'Clock Put up at Walter Slicers Sign of
the Spread Eagle [tavern]. Went to Samuel Smith Esquire to
deliver my letter of introduction, &c. he being out of Town at
his farm, gave me a Short period of time to make a Survey on
this place. The Town of Cumberland is a handsome little place
with many good brick buildings in the same, it is situated on
the North Branch of the River Potomac, Wills Creek a large
Stream of Water running through the Town (directly emptying
itself in the River) affords an opportunity for the erection of
several Merchant Mills, One large New Brick Mill looks well is
an acquisition to the place, is bounded in the front by Spurs of
the Alegany Mountain, on the rear, the right & the Left by those
Little Bull Dog Mountains, the whole Afford when on the
neighboring hills a pleasant lively romantick appearance (no
scarcity of Romanticks in this world).
    There is a handsome Bridge hung upon Chains which carry
over Wills Creek into the other part of Town [not the later
Narrows Bridge, built in 1833], directly ascending the Hill after
crossing bridge on an high yes very high Emminance stand the
ruins of the old fort (which takes the mind to Braddocks War)
it has full command of the river Down the same for a mile & up
about ½ a Mile, the river here makes a very quick short Bend
in the form of a horse Shoe, the fort directly standing on the
out side of the Shoe at the Toe of the same, which gives
command on both sides of the Shoe, or otherwise both up &
down the River...
    22nd of the Month & 7th of the Week [June 22]. This
morning set out from Cumberland and rode 5 Miles up the
Potomac & on the Cumberland Turnpike road to Carters at the
foot of the Aleghany Mountain fed & refreshed—$0.37½ [.]
Several little farms appears this far on the Potomac & amongst
the Hills: thence 16 miles on this Great Western Turnpike road
on the Allegheny mountain to Tomlinson's fed & dined—$0.68¾
thence 13 Miles to the Widow Janas and fed—0.12 ½ [.] this is
near Somerset County in State of Pennsylvania, thence in Somerset County 6 Miles to Phillip Smyth's Sine of General Jackson
[tavern] & Lodged; This great Turnpike road is far superior to
any of the Turnpike roads in Baltimore County for Masterly
Workmanship, the Bridges & Culverts actually do Credit to the

Executors of the same, the [Casselman River] Bridge over the Little Crossings of the Little Youghegany River is positively a Superb Bridge; The goodnes of God must have been in Congress unknownst to them; when the[y] fell about to & Erected a Lane for the making of this great Turnpike road which is the Salvation of those Mountains or Western Countrys & more benefit to the human family than Congress have any knowledge or any other Tribunal on the face of the Earth; I have seen no place on the Aleghany Mountain where they have Carried this road through but that has been done with as little Difficulty as making the Turn-pike Road up Joneses Falls, & one place in particular on this Mountain the road is carried on a Direct straight line for 3 Miles & I believe more & many other places from ½ a Mile to 1 & 2 Miles in a Strait line; this Great Western or Cumberland Turn Pike Road is free from Toll, it is not only good & handsome but is Ellegant & is & will be of more benefit than the Idea of man can possible have any knowledge of.

23rd of the month & 11th of the week [Sunday, June 23]. My Land Lord [tavern keeper] Phillip Smyth is a proud Empty Ignorant Rich Dutchman, Lives in a big wooden House with a Stone Chimney in each end, the house kept prodigeously Dirty; the living for man & horse is as good & looks as well as any of their Taverns, Inns or Hotels, he is situated Just on the East Side of the big Crossings of the Youghagany River in Somerset County, owns about 250 Acres of Land which he says that would sell for $50 pr Acre Just like a Top; he has Laid out a Town Just on the Bank of the River & directly on the Turnpike road which he calls Smyth-field and is now disposing of Lots some of them he says sells at $250 which is for ¼ of an Acre & fronting on the road (Baltimoreans Looke, Land Selling in the Middle of the Allegany mountains @ $1000 pr Acre) at this indended Town they have Commenced the erection of the Bridge over this River, no doubt but from the speciman of the work already on the road, but this Bridge will be a superb & Magnificent Building, this Mountain affords noble Stone for buildings & all that I have seen nearly of the same quality: when broken the grit looks like a rough Course Sande Stone.

Calls my Bill which is—$1.37½ [.]

Moves off & fords the River a Beautiful stream indeed, into Fayette county on General Braddock's old road 14 Miles to Freemans one hundred yards from this General Braddock was Interred. fed & Drank some Elegant Cyder—$0.37½ [.] thence 4 Miles to John Slack's very warm Stops to let [horse] Cate blow & Cool gives her a Gallon of Oats—$0.12½ [.] thence 6 Miles on & over Laurel hill to Union Town; on the top of Laurel Hill, about 3 Miles from Union Town; the Town & surrounding

Neighbor Hood affords a delightful Prospect indeed; leads the mind in spite of the Heart to contemplate the Promised Land that good old Moses was suffered to have a sight of but not to set his foot thereon after his Long and fatigueing Journey through the Wilderness.

I am now in Union Town formerly Beeson Town on the West Side of the Aleghany Mountain, the Back-Bone of America & Bug Bear of the World; Who piloted General Braddock so well through this Mountain 50 or 60 years ago; he from old England could never have had the opportunity to explore this Country & Carry this road through which bears the name of Braddocks Road even unto this day:

O the Traitorous Indians; some of them must have been his Guide; This great western Road is Carried and Laid out a great part of the way on the same Identical ground & totally carried through on the General direction of Braddocks road: This Mountain in Traveling through is but a mere flea bite to travel over, [compared] to the Mountains from Martinsburgh in [West] Virginia to Cumberland in Maryland at the foot of the Alleghany Mountain; It is true Braddocks road Is a rough & prodigiously stoney road, the stones principalley loose, but no worse than the same distance I have rode in many other parts of the world, if the same attention & Labour had been put on the road; it appears there is no roads mended or repaired on this Mountain if there is it is very little, the roads is no harder to keep up here than the roads in Baltimore or Chester Counties or of the County of Lancaster, they people are too abominably Lazy to repair roads here, Loose Stones & water running on the roads are the principal Evils; the Stones is very easy removed & that water would be easily turned off, but it gets liberty to run untill it makes Mires in the middle of the road & a Waggon will Swamp or Mire going down a Steep hill as well as going up.

If I had been Carried & set at Cartes which is said to be the foot of the Aleghany Mountain & known nothing About the Aleghany Mountain, I should have went on to Union Town & and pronounced the same to have been a poor stony rocky Country which abound plentifully with good Water, with an abundance of good Chestnut rail Timber, a great deal of Thin white oak Land with Grand White Oak trees on the same, & White or Spruce pines in Abundance, many very large & lofty. If not as lofty as the Cedars of Lebanon, they are as lofty as the Pines of the Aleghany: The Aleghany as well as its Surrounding Mountains ruined & kept poore by the raskally practice of seting fire to the same every 2 or 3 years; the persons that do it ought to be confined in the Mountains within the walls of a penitentiary built of the Materials they produce and fed on the beef of Rattle snakes & bears foot soop until the Great Masterly forests should Assume their natural & official Magnificence again: The destruction on this vast Extensive Aleghany forest done by fire, is not to be described with a pen: If this forest had never been fired it would have been a vast Large Extensive handsome Timbered Country, of Course the Land would have been thin, but it never would have Assumed the present horrid aspect which now prevail over the whole[.] I have rode through their Negro Mountains, their Shades of Death (here is the tall pines) their savage Mountains & many other desprate Mountains as they represent but I saw nothing so savage–like as many of the inhabitants thereof that appear in some degree like a part of the human race: If the fire could be stopped this part of the wourld would grow better.

In short 9 tenths of the people have no conception of the Alegheny Mountain that talks about it; the base false representations of it deceives the Idea of the mind & leads it to believe and conjecture Ideas that is Desperately Erronious: & many that see it speaks Erroniously of the same because they hear others at it.

Land genneraly sells on this vast great road through the Mountain for 10 to 50 Dollars per Acre & particular small pieces as much as 3 or 4 Acres in a piece at $100 pr Acre.

Union or Beeson Town is a Post & Country Town;... its situation is handsome & the surrounding neighborhood is a handsome hill Country in a good State of Cultivation; Red-Stone Creek runs through this Town which affords a Merchant Mill in the vicinity of the Town. I have put up at Thomas Brownfield sign of the Swan as soon as I came to Town which was yesterday 5 or six o'Clock.

6th Mo: 28th & 6th of the week [Friday, June 28]... The Barbers in this Country Visits the familys in the Town & precints came on to take the beard from Jacob [Beeson]: mine also was separated from my face for which I paid—$0.06¼ [.]

Baltimoreans would you believe that good old Jacob [Beeson] Living within two miles of the foot of Aleghany Mountain & on the West side of the same I mean his Estate two hundred thousand Dollars; at his request this day I wrote his Last Will & Testament which Satisfy's me in regard to his Estate.

[On to Brownsville, a journey recorded in only the briefest detail:]

Brownsville is situated amongst a Parcel of high & rapid Hills directly on the Banks of the Monogahela is coming to be a flourishing Town: Bridg-port is situated as Browns-ville coming to be a flourishing Town; A stranger would think no other than those two Towns were One & the same; Dunlops Creek running through sepearats those two Towns or Boroughs and emptys into the Monongahela, a bridge hung upon Chains over the Creek answers for & affords the communication from Town to Town: where the Post office stands, formerly stood Redstone fort which had command of the river for at least a mile up the same & but a short distance down (Red-Stone R. Creek emptyes in to the River in Sight below Brownsville) Sets upon the highest hill Just back of Town, has a full & beautiful view of Laurel hill at the distance of 14 Miles as well as a great part of Red-Stone, this Eminence gives the Sight full command of the river for 2 miles up & down, as well as many miles over the River to the West: Those hills in Town & near the same are full of Coal was introduced by a young Man who was my guide in to a Coal-pit, that led in horizontally had many turnings & windings, & the earth & rocks above from 20 to 30 feet thick supported & kept up by having Collumns of Stone coal for the same to rest on. when at the farthermost Side, 23 paces or 249 feet in a straight direction carried me Out; this Cave had a masterly & superb appearance, the pasages or streets in this pit let a Cart & horse in with Ease & when Loaded goes out easyly. Affords Coal in Abundance of an excellent quality...

Browns-ville & Bridge-port will become an Extensive place of trade & a flourishing town with Extensive Manufactorys of different kinds in the same, the Author of all goodness has Blessed those Hills on which this Town stands form the foundation of the World to the present time, & will yet continue to bless it for Ages to Come.

ADLARD WELBY, 1819

By Dearborn Wagon, Western Pennsylvania to Wheeling / Washington to Cumberland

[Western Pennsylvania, late August, traveling westbound in a light, four-wheel Dearborn wagon followed by his servant in a covered baggage wagon. He began his trip in New York July 6.]

From the slight chirping of a few grasshoppers or crickets in England, no one can have a conception of the noise of a summer night here; all the insect tribe seem to open at once and to join in one perpetual chorus, very unpleasant to ears unaccustomed to it.

The Pensilvanians resemble in many points the Scots: they go barefoot, they have both some dirty habits, neither have yet very generally erected temples to Cloacina beyond the immediate neighbourhood of great towns. A medical man lately told me that the itch, a disorder which proves uncleanliness where it prevails, was as rife as in Scotland; of drams of whisky and bitters they are equally fond. In cookery the comparison turns in favour of our northern neighbours, who understand it far better than they do here, where it is the most abominable messing and spoiling of provision imaginable: nothing but frying in butter till the stomach turns even at the smell; of vegetables they have but small variety, and of these these the sickly tasting beet is a favourite, which they dress in the same disgusting way as the fleshmeat, neither good for palate or stomach.

A black girl with youthful spirits was playing with a lad in the town street [unidentified town in western Pennsylvania], when the wheelwright, with whom I was talking while he mended the carriage, said, "if it were not for fear of the law one would be inclined to put an end to that black——; they ought to be taught the difference between a black and a white, and to pay more respect than to think of associating with them!" The man spoke really in earnest, and would have thought little of putting the girl to death.

Immediately afterwards I met a white little boy who followed a tall mulatto woman, and with all his little strength was beating her with a stick; at length the woman could bear it no longer, and told him, if she should be *whipped* the next moment for it, she would pull his ears if he continued to do so.

On leaving Washington [Pennsylvania] a few miles, the traveler enters the state of Virginia, which he crosses to Wheeling, a town on the eastern bank of the Ohio. The whole way is in general a fine drive, and in two or three years will be better from the improved roads forming everywhere as we pass with great judgment and spirit. The National road is a work truly worthy of a great nation, both in its idea and construction; upon it, the traveller will be enabled to pass with comfort, from the eastern coast, westward . . .

Almost all the labourers employed here upon the roads are either Irish or English, and it is not certain that these republicans have not a secret pride in beholding the natives of the old world toiling for their benefit; however, the earnings of the men are I believe sufficient to render them in time independent, and I must say they look in general well fed, well clothed and comfortable. We passed one party employed in ploughing down part of the uneven road with a strong machine drawn by eight oxen, while two others drew a large wooden scoop to shovel up and lead away the ploughed up soil; it appeared to save much labour. The Irish here have not lost in our esteem; two or three times we have been beholden to individuals of that nation for good-natured little services: one of them lately aided me successfully to get along part of the new road where we had met with some opposition; another actually accompanied us about nine miles on a like occasion, not with a view to remuneration, for I could not persuade him to take any thing for his services but some refreshment at the tavern. I heartily return them the good wishes they so frequently expressed as we passed them. One of the above men had acquired some property; he told me that seven years ago he bought land at six dollars per acre, and that he had just sold a part of it at fifty, and some even so high as seventy dollars per acre. The proximity of the new road had increased thus the value of his land.

Where, or when an American uses water for the purpose of washing more than his face and fingers, does not appear, for no water ever goes up stairs at a tavern unless your own servants take it. Under the shed of the house, water and tin basons are placed in the morning, and each one on coming down rubs his face and hands over;—they may bathe perhaps in rivers occasionally; if not, they are a decidedly dirty people. An English youth at our inn at Wheeling in order to wash himself a little more effectually, let his shirt down to his waistband; an attempt at cleanliness so unusual caused a general surprise and laugh among the *yahoos.* ...

[*From Wheeling, Welby traveled through Ohio, Kentucky, and Indiana, returning to Wheeling and the National Road in late October 1819—as usual, recording his observations in great detail but often omitting places names and only rarely recording the day of the week. We rejoin him in Washington in early November.*]

We stayed a day at Washington, Pensilvania, comfortably received at Mr. Morris's good tavern, and then took a new route [the National Road] by the south-west corner of this State: crossing the Monongahela river we baited at Brownsville, at an excellent house kept by Mr. Evans, an emigrant; from thence, by a fine new road [the same] through Union Town, we soon entered the picturesque State of Maryland, and arrived at a small town called Fort Cumberland. The traveler by this route will pass the mountains scarcely knowing it, except from the fine views of the subjacent country which are frequently presented to view; that from the top of the hill about eleven or twelve miles west of Cumberland is truly magnificent. Along this

Wheeling, 1941: a recently widened and repaved section of the National
Road.

well-formed road we pass without once being stopped to pay toll, and I understood it to be the intention of the United States government to finish and support this western road...

The reader will be mistaken if, from what has been said of good roads and fine weather, he suposes we meet with nothing else; from a few miles off Wheeling until this day or two, the air has been filled with what in England would be thought a thick fog,—here they say it is smoke arising from burning barrens and prairies which are yearly at this time set on fire; indeed we have lately passed near enough to woodland on fire to see the flames and to hear the crackling of the timber; to our eyes a melancholy sight, accustomed as they have been to value and admire the forest growth.

Within this week a considerable number of waggons laden with goods and people have passed on their way to the Western country: as this Indian summer cannot last much longer, these parties would seem to be some of the improvident of the earth not to have moved earlier to their destination.

JAMES HALL, 1820
By Wagon, Cumberland and Vicinity

James Hall

This section of the road, which embraces the Allegheny mountains, has since been completed, in a manner which reflects the highest credit upon those engaged in its construction. It is a permanent turnpike, built of stone, and covered with gravel, so as to unite solidity and smoothness; and noble arches of stone have been thrown, at a vast expense, over all the ravines and water-courses. In some places the road is hewn into the precipitous side of the mountain, and the traveller, beholding a vast abyss beneath his feet, while the tall cliffs rising to the clouds overhang his path, is struck with admiration at the bold genius which devised, and the persevering hardihood which executed, so great a work. Those frightful precipices, which once almost defied the approach of the nimble footed hunter, are now traversed by heavy laden wagons; and pleasure carriages roll rapidly along where beasts of prey but lately found a secure retreat. Another appropriation has since been made to extend this road to Zanesville in Ohio; and commissioners have been appointed to survey and trace out its route to the shores of the Mississippi.

Cumberland is a pretty little town, delightfully situated on a branch of the Potomac, and in one of those romantic spots which are often found in mountainous and secluded situations.

Braddock assembled his army here, at the commencement of the celebrated campaign which ended in his defeat and death; and he passed the mountains by nearly the same route which has been selected for the national road. This path was traced by an Indian guide, who, with that instinctive acuteness for which the whole race is remarkable, added, no doubt, to a intimate knowledge of the country, at once struck out the very course which the experience of half a century has proved to be the best and shortest.

A ROAD "RAPIDLY IMPAIRED"

"Best and shortest"... yet the road had hardly been built when it began to deteriorate—in some places rapidly. In part, this was because of how the road was constructed: it was basically a trench sunk into the ground, filled first with large stone and then a layer of small stone, which made it prone to collect water, causing the larger stone to sink and, in winter, making the whole road heave and often become impassable. In places, only a single layer of stone had been laid. Another reason was the nature of the traffic: the swiftly moving wheels of coaches tended to scatter the surface stone, while the slower-moving wheels of much more heavily laden wagons tended to make ruts. And then there was the fact that the road had been built in sections by different contractors who varied in capability and conscientiousness. And, of course, the terrain: those steep slopes down which water cascaded over the road, followed by loosened earth and rocks. But most of all, the road was simply getting far heavier use than had been anticipated.

The deteriorating condition of the road was striking. "In some places," said one early observer, "the bed of the road is cut through by wheels, making cavities which continually increase and retain water, which, by softening the road, contribute to the enlargement of the cavities. In others, the road is much impaired by the sliding down of the earth and rocks from the elevated hills." Another traveler found the ruts "worn so broad and deep by heavy travel that an army of pigmies might march into the bosom of the country under the cover they would afford."

The federal government was not oblivious; but while there had been agreement on the constitutionality of building *the road there was not, rather incongruously, on the constitutionality of* maintaining *it. The most expedient method would have been to turn the National Road into a toll road. There were* many such roads of state or private jurisdiction. But a bill to do so was vetoed in 1822 by President Monroe on the grounds that the Constitution did not give the federal government the authority to build toll houses and collect tolls—indeed, that it did not even allow for federal maintenance of the road the federal government had built. The following year an appropriation for repairs became law, but it was only for $25,000.

In 1826, with the road worse still, the House committee on roads and canals proposed new legislation. Pennsylvania Representative Andrew Stewart observed in a speech to the House March 3, 1826:

> At present this road, owing to the great and increasing travel upon it, its total neglect, and exposure to the destructive operation of the elements, is in a state of rapid dilapidation, and unless some remedy be soon applied, total destruction must be the speedy and inevitable result; by which the government will not only lose this magnificent national work, with all its numerous and important advantages, but also the immense sums of money expended in its construction.... Without this right [to maintain the road], the power to construct is nugatory and ineffectual."

But Stewart's exhortation was to no avail. The road, for the time, remained toll-free and scarcely maintained.

* * *

William Blane, an English gentleman on a trip through the United States and Canada in 1822, found the road between Brownsville and Wheeling "very much out of repair" just four years after that section had been completed. Later that year, at the behest of Congress, Postmaster General R. J. Meigs, Jr., personally inspected the entire length of the road to assess the effect of its condition on "the safe and speedy transportation of the United States' mail" and declared parts of the road to be in "a ruinous state." A few years later, the road was still "awful," in the opinion of Charles Fenno Hoffman, later an associate of Horace Greeley.

WILLIAM BLANE, 1822
By Stagecoach, Cumberland to Wheeling

[October 1822]
Leaving Cumberland, I proceeded on the great National Road which crosses the Alleghany Mountains, and which reaches from Cumberland to Wheeling, a distance of 125 miles. The road begins to ascend almost immediately, and passes through a

rough and mountainous country, thickly covered with forest, which is chiefly oak, here and there interspersed with pine and cedar. The underwood is generally very thick, the spare ground between the trees being covered with large mountain Laurel (Kalmia Latifolia). This is so abundant and luxuriant in some places, that the woods seem almost impenetrable. Deer, bears, wolves, wild turkies, and indeed all kinds of wild animals, are uncommonly plentiful in these mountains, owing to the rocky nature of the ground, which will in all probability prevent its being cultivated for centuries.

While the stage was stopping a short time in order to water the horses, and to allow the passengers to take some refreshment at a small inn on this mountain, I observed that two hunters, who had just come in with some turkies they had killed, were each of them carrying one of the long heavy rifles peculiar to the Americans. As one of them, an old man, was boasting of his skill as a marksman, I offered to put up a half-dollar at a distance of fifty yards, to be his if he could hit it. Accordingly I stepped the distance, and placed the half-dollar in the cleft of a small stick, which I thrust into the ground. The hunter, slowly raising his rifle, fired, and to my great astonishment struck the half-dollar. This was the first specimen I had seen, of the unrivalled accuracy with which the American hunter uses his rifle, and which I had afterwards still greater reason to be surprised at when in Kentucky.

On the road I met vast droves of hogs, four or five thousand in a drove, going from the State of Ohio across the mountains to the Eastern States. Afterwards, when in Kentucky, I was informed that upwards of 100,000 hogs had been driven from that State alone. Owing to the quantity of nuts, acorns, and mast, throughout the Western States, a great number of these animals are allowed to run at large in the woods, are bred at little or no expense, and when fat are sold in the Eastern States for about five dollars a-piece.

The road became worse and worse all the way from Brownsville to Wheeling. The truth is, that as travellers coming from the Atlantic cities, with the intention of descending the Ohio and going into the Western States, prefer this road to the one which leads from Philadelphia to Pittsburgh, and which was made by the State of Pennsylvania, the traffic of the Pennsylvanian "turnpike" is very much diminished; and therefore all the people of that State, as well as of many of the other States, who do not derive any immediate benefit from it, are opposed to any grants being made by Congress for keeping it [the National Road] in order. Thus, for the want of a few thousand dollars expended annually, this great national undertaking was allowed to go very much

The stage wagon, an early form of the stagecoach, had backless bench
seats. It was popular in the late 1700s and early 1800s until replaced
by the more familiar Concord coach.

"On the road I met vast droves of hogs, four or five thousand in a drove."—William Blane

Hogs, sheep, cattle and other livestock could be bred cheaply in the Midwest and sold in the East for a substantial profit. The most practical means of transportation was on-the-hoof.

Harper's Magazine, November 1879

out of repair. It would indeed in a year or two have become entirely impassable if, as I was informed on my return from the West, the advocates for internal improvements had not made a great effort, and obtained a grant of 25,000 dollars. This however is by no means enough for repairing the road at present, whereas a few years ago the same sum would have been more than sufficient.

Wheeling is situated on the left bank of the Ohio, at the foot of a very high cliff. I found it but a small town, and owing to its manufactures extremely dirty; but it is soon likely to become a place of considerable importance, from the great quantity of merchandise brought to and from the Ohio along the National Road.

R. J. MEIGS, JR, 1822
On Horseback, Cumberland to Wheeling

R.J. Meigs, Jr.

[Written in 1823 as a report to Congress]
In obedience to a resolution of the House of Representatives, passed the 31st of December, relating to the state and condition of the Cumberland [or National] road, the obstacles (existing) to the safe and speedy transportation of the United States' mail on said road, and what effect they may have (if not removed) on the expenditure of the Post Office Department, I have the honor to communicate: That, in the month of November last, I passed over the whole of that road, and, traveling only by day-light, was enabled to observe its state and condition, which I attentively did.

The western (being the newest) part of the road is in a ruinous state, and becoming rapidly impaired.

In some places the bed of the road is cut through by wheels, making cavities which continually increase and retain water, which, by softening the rock, contribute to the enlargement of the cavities. In others, the road is much impaired by the sliding down of the earth and rocks from the elevated hills; and by the falling off of parts of the road down steep and precipitous declivities of several hundred feet; so much abridging the width of the road that two carriages cannot pass each other.

Obstacles do really exist to the safe and speedy transportation of the United States' mail upon that road. The mail contractors have sometimes been necesitated to remove them before the mails could pass on; and such delay produced, that the mail stages have, in some instances, been unable to reach their point of arrival in due season to deliver over the mail, and, consequently, producing failures.

The Overland Mail. A wood engraving in *Frank Leslie's Illustrated Newspaper,* 1858.

If these obstacles are suffered to exist and increase, the great western mail must be transported on lengthier, oblique, and circuitous roads, which will retard the expedition of the mail, and considerably enhance the expenditure of the Post Office Department.

The Cumberland road, so interesting to the nation, will, (in my opinion, formed by observation when upon it) cease to be useful unless repaired. That part of the road contiguous to Cumberland, and the oldest, is in a tolerably good condition, because it has been seasonably and judiciously repaired; which repair was true economy in the preservation of the road.

CHARLES FENNO HOFFMAN, 1833
On Horseback, Washington to Wheeling

[Approaching Washington, Pennsylvania, in late October after traveling from New York via Easton, Harrisburg, Bedford, and Somerset]

About thirty miles from Wheeling we first struck the national road. It appears to have been originally constructed of large round stones, thrown without much arrangement on the surface of the soil, after the road was first levelled. These are now being ploughed up, and a thin layer of broken stones is in many places spread over the renovated surface. I hope the roadmakers have not the conscience to call this Macadamizing. It yields like snow-drift to the heavy wheels which traverse it, and the very best parts of the road that I saw are not to be compared with a Long Island turnpike. Two-thirds indeed of the extent we traversed were worse than any artificial road I ever travelled, except perhaps the log causeways among the new settlements in northern New-York. The ruts are worn so broad and deep by heavy travel, that an army of pigmies might march into the bosom of the country under the cover they would afford; and old Ixion himself could hardly trundle his wheel over such awful furrows. Perhaps I was the more struck with the appearance of this celebrated highway from the fact of much of the road over the mountains having been in excellent condition. There is one feature, however, in this national work which is truly fine—I allude to the massive stone bridges which form a part of it. They occur, as the road crosses a winding creek, a dozen times within twice as many miles. They consist either of one, two, or three arches; the centre arch being sprung a foot or two higher than those on either side. Their thick walls projecting above the road, their round stone buttresses, and

Charles Fenno Hoffman

Library of Congress

carved key-stones combine to give them an air of Roman solidity and strength. They are monuments of taste and power that will speak well for the country when the brick towns they bind together shall have crumbled in the dust.

These frequently recurring bridges are striking objects in the landscape, where the road winds many miles through a narrow valley. They may be seen at almost every turn spanning the deep bosom of the defile, and reflected with all their sombre beauty in the stream below.

The valley widens within a few miles of Wheeling, and the road strikes into the hill-side, whose crooked base it has long been following. It soon begins to be cut out of the solid rock, and the ascent is rapidly accelerated. Above, on the right, the trees impend from a lofty hill over your path, and far below you see the stream, so long your companion, gleaming through a small cultivated bottom, which shows like a garden to the eye. It is girdled by steep hills, and seems, with its single mill and one or two farm-houses, to be shut out from all the world. Advance but a pistol-shot, and you look into the chimneys of Wheeling. The Ohio is beneath your feet. The town lies in so narrow a strip along the river, that, from the ridge on which you stand, you will hardly notice its crowded buildings. That first view of the lovely river of the west is worth a journey of a thousand miles. The clear majestic tide, the fertile islands on its bosom, the bold and towering heights opposite, with the green esplanade of alluvion in front, and the forest-crowned headlands above and below, round which the river sweeps away, to bless and gladden the fruitful regions that drink its limpid waters— these, with the recollections of deeds done upon its banks—the wild incidents and savage encounters of border story, so immediately contrasted with all the luxuries of civilization that now float securely upon that peaceful current—these make up a moral picture whose colours are laid in the heart, never to be effaced. No man will ever forget his first view of the Ohio.

I passed an evening most agreeably at Wheeling, with two or three prominent members of the Bar, who were distinguished by that courtesy and cordial frankness which mark the western Virginian. A venison steak and flask of old Tuscaloosa (the relish and flavour of which would have been tocsin to the soul of Apicius, and made Anacreon uneasy in his grave) gave cordiality to the meeting. It was my first introduction into western society, and I could hardly have been initiated under better auspices, as I went under the wing of an Ohio gentleman, whose warm hospitality and endearing social qualities, united as they are to distinguished professional talents, seem to make him a universal favourite in this region. The conversation animated, various, and instructive, would supply material for a dozen letters. But the nervous expressions, and almost startling boldness, of western phraseology would lose half its vividness and power when transferred to paper.

Wheeling is one of the most flourishing places on the Ohio. The immense quantity of bituminous coal in the adjacent region, which may be had merely for the digging, gives it great advantages as a manufacturing place, while the rich back country and favourable position on the river, especially in low water, when steamboats find Pittsburgh difficult of access, make the town a place of active trade.

The principal tavern of the place, wherein I lodged, is well supplied with bedchambers, and parlours, and a comfortable reading-room, where the leading papers in the Union are taken. The attendance too, all the servants being blacks, is very good. Among them, a perfect treasure, in the shape of a genuine old Virginia negro, must not be forgotten. The features of Billy (for that is the name of my sable friend) are an exact copy of those generally introduced into Washington's picture when he is painted with his favourite groom in attendance. I piqued myself considerably upon having discovered the likeness, when I afterward found that the worthy Ethiop had actually been "raised," as he expressed it, in the Washington family.

It was with no slight regret that I parted with my friend S. [not otherwise identified], when stepping on board a pretty steamboat, called the Gazelle, to take my passage up the river [to Pittsburgh]; his foreign travel, and various opportunities, have given him habits of observation which, with a dash of humour and ready flow of fine spirits, constitute a capital traveling companion. I left him waiting for the downward boat, and we parted, promising to meet again in a few months at New-Orleans—each of us in the mean time traversing regions from which the kingdoms and principalities of Europe might be carved out and never missed.

III. THE ROAD IN ITS HEYDAY

*Recollections of the busiest years
by some of those who lived them*

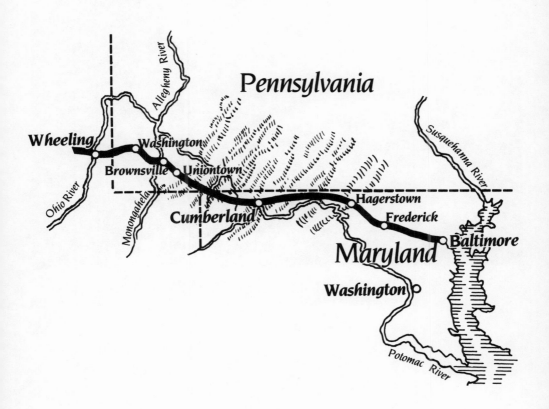

The spirit of the National Road in its heyday.

THE GLORY YEARS

In its heyday—roughly through the 1840s—the National Road was by all accounts the busiest in the land. Some "cavities," "declivities," and "awful furrows" notwithstanding, it was travelable, and travel it the nation did.

By fast-flying stagecoach, gaily painted; or heavy-laden Conestoga, canvas flapping; by twelve-horse freight wagon, axles creaking; or swift, robust horse, or plodding mule, or carriage, or Dearborn wagon, or even hired hack...

A traveler on foot, a band of gypsies, a circus caravan...

East went west....

Through apple orchards and fields of Indian corn, through meadows of timothy, and hollows of oak, chestnut, and wildflowers... up, up, the slopes... of pine and mountain laurel... then steeper slopes, and pine immense in height now... to a glorious view of "the Promised Land," as the world beyond the Alleghenies looked to one traveler.

They came. And the road made them welcome. Where once travelers sought mountain springs for drink and wild game for food and a broad tree or a hunter's hut for shelter, now inns and taverns offered a bed and a good meal; where once only the stout-hearted ventured in the footprints of Indians, now stagecoach lines made travel possible for all.

Inns—or taverns, as they were commonly called when they also sold liquor—cropped up as quickly as the road went by. These, now, were mostly built for the purpose. In the days of Braddock's Road there were one or two inns worthy of the name over the whole road—Tomlinson's, for example, which, when rebuilt as the National Road came through, was perhaps

"Many of the most illustrious statesmen and heroes of the early period of our national existence passed over the National Road. The writer remembers with no little pride shaking hands with General Jackson."—Thomas Searight

Andrew Jackson at a stagecoach stop during the heyday of the National Road.

Harper's Weekly, March 12, 1881. Illustration by Howard Pyle.

its most famous. But for the most part travelers had to make do with whatever simple accommodations they could find at a private home—sometimes just a bed in some settler's cabin.

The taverns of the National Road usually had sleeping quarters on the second floor, and sometimes a third, dormitory-style; the first floor had its dining area, with long, often common tables at which a traveling congressman might partake side by side with a stagecoach driver. There was inevitably a bar, well stocked with whiskey that sold almost as cheaply as water. Tavern keepers usually sought no profit on sales of liquor; they kept it available, at cost, for the accommodation of guests. Fare frequently served included hot biscuits, venison cutlets, ham and eggs, roast chicken, johnnycakes, waffles, and such game as quail, pheasant, grouse, rabbit, squirrel, wild turkey, and salted bear meat; or fresh trout or perch from a mountain stream—and even fresh oysters from Maryland, shipped as far west as Ohio in good weather by a stage company known as the "Oyster Line," which presumably took along passengers as well. And there were fresh vegetables and fruits of the season. Breakfast often consisted of sausage and buckwheat cakes with maple syrup. Ham and eggs (especially fine-flavored, home-cured Pennsylvania ham) was often served for dinner as well as breakfast, and was the choice of Andrew Jackson dining in Uniontown on the way to his inauguration. Taverns varied in quality, but on the whole they had the reputation of being clean and well maintained, serving food that, while often plain, was abundant and well cooked.

Early taverns had names reminiscent of old England—the Black Horse, the White Swan, and so on. By the heyday, the practice was often to associate the tavern with some well-known personage—hence the General Jackson, the Benjamin Franklin, the Washington, and so on—or to make a relatively well-known personage out of the owner of the tavern, as for example (Jesse) Tomlinson's, (Evan) Gwinn's, and (William) Searight's.

Often the tavern was also the stage office, selling tickets and keeping schedules available. Stagecoaches were the way to go—for those who could afford them. They were quick, for competition forced the fastest possible service, and stage drivers sometimes spent ten to twelve consecutive hours behind the whip. They were relatively luxurious, some coaches being lined with purple silk or red damask, while nearly all were ornately painted and prominently lettered in gold with the name of the stage line (Stockton's, the Good Intent, the Landlord's, the June Bug, the Citizens', the People's). The stagecoaches were fairly expensive—more than many a traveler could afford:

Some of the old road's taverns have been restored to their old use; but only one, so far as is known, has been in continuous use since the National Road began, and indeed even before. Travelers have been eating in this same room of the Century Inn in Scenery Hill, Pennsylvania, since 1794, when the tavern was established by Stephen Hill.

a one-way fare from Baltimore to Wheeling was $17.50; subfares were $2 between Frederick and Hagerstown and $4 between Cumberland and Uniontown. By another line, Zanesville to Columbus was $2 and took eight hours; Cumberland to Indianapolis was $18.25.

The early stagecoaches were essentially wagons with board seats, usually three, fitted across. By the 1830s, the more familiar Concord coach became the mainstay of travel.

Slower but infinitely more practical for the westbound pioneer was the Conestoga wagon, which could pack enough household possessions, clothing, blankets, and the like for setting up house on the frontier. As long as 26 feet, with huge wheels as great as 10 feet in diameter and 10 inches in width, they had enormous capacity—fitted for transportation of freight they could carry up to five tons. Their canvas tops drawn over wooden bows provided protection from the elements and a relatively snug place for sleeping. Traveling time was about 18 to 20 miles a day except for the steepest ascents of the Alleghenies. But many a western-bound pioneer was too poor to afford a state-of-the-art Conestoga. The National Road also was full of little one-horse wagons plenty big enough to haul all that such people had to take with them.

Perhaps the most exciting moments on the road in its heyday were the chances of seeing up close, and occasionally shaking hands with, some of the most famous people of the day. President Andrew Jackson was a frequent traveler. James Polk, like Jackson, used the road on the way to his inauguration, and James Monroe, John Quincy Adams, Martin Van Buren, William Henry Harrison, Zachary Taylor, Millard Fillmore, James Buchanan, and Abraham Lincoln traveled it at various times. Henry Clay regularly took the road on his way to and from sessions of Congress. Sam Houston, John C. Calhoun, Daniel Webster, John C. Fremont, and James G. Blaine used it, as did Davy Crockett. Celebrities like Jenny Lind and Phineas T. Barnum were also National Road travelers—Barnum with a ten-horse entourage.

As a single national avenue showing off its national heroes, the National Road was perhaps unequaled by any one road since the Appian Way's triumphal processions of consuls and proconsuls. Indeed, the National Road was often equated with that national road of ancient Rome.

"I look upon it . . . as a monument which will be regarded by those who come after us with the same enthusiasm with which the classic scholar now looks to the Appian way," extolled Representative Ogden Hoffman in Congress in 1840. And it wasn't a matter of parochial pride—Hoffman was from New York. The National Road is "the pride of the country," boasted

Other of the old taverns have gone the way of oblivion. Colley's, in Brier Hill, Pennsylvania, built in 1796, sits empty and forlorn, little by little becoming one with the elements of wood and earth and stone from which it was created. Its front door, which once swung open welcomingly to travelers of old, now is fixed shut, its "No Trespassing" sign a sharp reminder of its demise.

the distinguished orator Edward Everett, of Massachusetts. It
was truly a national symbol.

In drawing the analogy with ancient Rome, Hoffman might
have gone further, for the parallels are many. The United States,
in the early days of the Republic, had a fondness for things
Roman. The founding fathers went back to Rome for the terms
"capitol" and "senate." Architectural independence was declared by turning sharply from the Georgian of colonial days to
the trend setter of the first half of the nineteenth century, the
classical revival. All was summed up in the Great Seal's Latin
inscription, *Novus Ordo Seclorum*—A New Order Among the
Ages.

In the National Road, the United States recreated essential
qualities of the remarkable road system of ancient Rome, which,
until the nineteenth century, remained the greatest road network the world had ever known. The Roman road system grew,
first of all, out of political considerations. It was a strategic
network by which the central government could maintain its
control over far-flung territories, carrying the emperor's legions
by the shortest and quickest route when it was necessary to
maintain that control by force. The National Road was also a
political creation, intended to maintain close ties between the
government in the east and the emerging states and territories
of the west. Appropriately, the road of ancient Rome was a
creation of the central government; so, too, the National Road—
the only American road ever built directly by the federal
government.

The Roman road builder made every effort to construct his
road in as straight a line as possible, and his road network was
renowned for its straightness. The builders of the National Road
were under Congressional directive to build it according to
"the least distance of road"—or straightest route. This was in
marked contrast to the road that had evolved thus far in
America, the road that meandered around obstacles or circled
about for the easiest river crossing—the road as it also existed
throughout the world from the decline of the Roman empire
into the nineteenth century.

Finally, of course, there were those "noble arches of stone"
on the National Road, looking like nothing so much as Roman
antiquities.

* * *

Among the many chroniclers of the road, none perhaps knew it
better than Tom Searight, who as a boy shook hands with
Andrew Jackson when the president traveled the road to Washington. Searight's father was a contractor for some of the road's

"*The sign-boards of National Road taverns were elevated upon high
and heavy posts, and their golden letters, winking in the sun, ogled
the wayfarer from the hot road-bed and gave promise of good cheer.*"
—Thomas Searight

Above: Frostburg, Maryland.

construction and for many years was a National Road commissioner for the state of Pennsylvania. Tom Searight was a lawyer, but he is best remembered as a raconteur of the National Road.

Still another chronicler of the same period was William H. Wills, an itinerant Methodist preacher from North Carolina, who traveled the road in 1840.

THOMAS B. SEARIGHT, 1830s–1850s
Personal Recollections, Uniontown

Thomas B. Searight

Searight, *The Old Pike*

From the time it was thrown open to the public, in the year 1818, until the coming of the railroads west of the Allegheny mountains in 1852, the National Road was the one great highway, over which passed the bulk of trade and travel, and the mails between the East and the West. Its numerous and stately stone bridges with handsomely turned arches, its iron mile posts and its old iron gates, attest the skill of the workmen engaged on its construction, and to this day remain enduring monuments of its grandeur and solidity, all save the imposing iron gates, which have disappeared by process of conversion prompted by some utilitarian idea, savoring in no little measure of sacrilege.

Many of the most illustrious statesmen and heroes of the early period of our national existence passed over the National Road from their homes to the capital and back, at the opening and closing of the sessions of Congress. Jackson, Harrison, Clay, Sam Houston, Polk, Taylor, Crittenden, Shelby, Allen, Scott, Butler, the eccentric Davy Crockett, and many of their contemporaries in public service, were familiar figures in the eyes of the dwellers by the roadside. The writer of these pages frequently saw these distinguished men on their passage over the road, and remembers with no little pride the incident of shaking hands with General Jackson, as he sat in his carriage on the wagon-yard of an old tavern. A coach, in which Mr. Clay was proceeding to Washington, was upset on a pile of limestone, in the main street of Uniontown, a few moments after supper at the McClelland house. Sam Sibley was the driver of that coach, and had his nose broken by the accident. Mr. Clay was unhurt, and upon being extricated from the grounded coach, facetiously remarked that: "This is mixing the Clay of Kentucky with the limestone of Pennsylvania."

As many as twenty four-horse coaches have been counted in line at one time on the road, and large, broad-wheeled wagons, covered with white canvass stretched over bows, laden with merchandise and drawn by six Conestoga horses, were visible all the day long at every point, and many times until late in the evening, besides innumerable caravans of horses, mules, cattle, hogs and sheep. It looked more like the leading avenue of a great city than a road through rural districts.

The road had a peculiar nomenclature, familiar to the tens of thousands who traveled over it in its palmy days. The names, for example, applied to particular localities on the line, are of striking import, and blend harmoniously with the unique history of the road. With these names omitted, the road would be robbed of much that adds interest to its history. Among the best remembered of these are, The Shades of Death, The Narrows, Piney Grove, Big Crossings, Negro Mountain, Keyser's Ridge, Woodcock Hill, Chalk Hill, Big Savage, Little Savage, Snake Hill, Laurel Hill, The Turkey's Nest, Egg Nog Hill, Coon Island and Wheeling Hill. Rich memories cluster around every one of these names, and old wagoners and stage drivers delight to linger over the scenes they bring to mind.

The road was justly renowned for the great number and excellence of its inns or taverns. On the mountain division, every mile had its tavern. Here one could be seen perched on some elevated site, near the roadside, and there another, sheltered behind a clump of trees, many of them with inviting seats for idlers, and all with cheerful fronts toward the weary traveler. The sign-boards were elevated upon high and heavy posts, and their golden letters winking in the sun, ogled the wayfarer from the hot road-bed and gave promise of good cheer, while the big trough, overflowing with clear, fresh water, and the ground below it sprinkled with droppings of fragrant peppermint, lent a charm to the scene that was well nigh enchanting.

The great majority of taverns were called wagon stands, because their patrons were largely made up of wagoners, and each provided with grounds called the wagon-yard, whereon teams were driven to feed, and rest over night. The very best of entertainment was furnished at these wagon stands. The taverns where stage horses were kept and exchanged, and stage passengers took meals, were called "stage houses," located at intervals of about twelve miles, as nearly as practicable.

The beer of the present day was unknown, or if known, unused on the National Road during the era of its prosperity. Ale was used in limited quantities, but was not a favorite drink. Whisky was the leading beverage, and it was plentiful and cheap. The price of a drink of whisky was three cents, except at the stage houses, where by reason of an assumption of aristocracy the price was five cents. The whisky of that day is said to have been pure, and many persons of unquestioned respectability affirm with much earnestness that it never produced delirium tremens. The current coin of the road was the big copper cent of United States coinage, the "fippenny bit," Spanish, of the value of six and one-fourth cents, called for brevity a "fip," the "levy," Spanish, of the value of twelve and a half cents, the quarter, the half dollar, and the dollar. The Mexican and Spanish milled dollar were oftener seen than the United States dollar. The silver five-cent piece and the dime of the United States coinage were seen occasionally, but not so much used as the "fip" and the "levy." In times of stringency, the stage companies issued scrip in denominations ranging from five cents to a dollar, which passed readily for money. The scrip was similar to the postal currency of the war period, lacking only in the artistic skill displayed in the engraving of the latter. A hungry traveler could obtain a substantial meal at an old wagon stand tavern for a "levy," and two drinks of whisky for a "fippenny bit." The morning bill of a wagoner with a six-horse team did not exceed one dollar and seventy-five cents, which included grain and hay for the horses, meals for the driver, and all the drinks he saw proper to take.

WILLIAM H. WILLS, 1840

By Stagecoach, Cumberland to Wheeling

[*Leaving home in Tarboro, North Carolina, April 1, 1840, Wills traveled by carriage and rail to Baltimore (via Richmond and Washington), and then took the Baltimore and Ohio Railroad west to Frederick, Maryland. There he switched to a stagecoach, arriving in Hancock, Maryland, at 8 a.m. Saturday, April 4.*]

From Hancock we reached Cumberland, 40 miles from the former, at 5 o'clock P.M. Cumberland is a very pretty place of about 3000 inhabitants and some five or six churches. Here begins the famous Cumberland Road, began and continued on by the U.S. government. It was commenced about 30 or 35 years ago and almost every year has been a subject of debate in Congress. Still appropriations have been annually made until the road has been carried thro' Wheeling, Va., to Zanesville, Ohio, 75 ms from Whl. and the whole length about 200 ms. It is macadamized and is indeed one of the finest roads in the U.S., being always good whether winter or summer. From Balt. to Cumberland the road has also been finished in the same style but not so perfect, by private enterprise. This road is of immense advantage especially to stages and waggons the latter of which are capable of drawing on it with their 6 horse teams

6 tons. It is indeed the grand throughfare between the west &
Balt. and I suppose on the course of the route I must have seen
an hundred, perhaps an hundred and fifty, heavy waggons
loaded with produce and merchandise.

From Cumberland we rode to a little village called Frostburg
where we got a most excellent supper at 7 o'clock. The fare on
this road is good and marked by the same peculiarity attending
the inhabitants in the mountainous districts of No. Ca[rolina], that
is a fondness for Coffee and sweet things for dinner, and pickles
and preserves for breakfast. About 12 o'clock at night we
stopped upon the highest point of the Cumberland Mountains
and put out two ladies and a little child who had traveled with
us from Hancock. The mother kept a public house upon the
very top. During the night I had my curtains and windows
down, and they sat with theirs open enjoying the mountain
breeze. "And are you not very cold on that hill in winter"? said
I. "Oh no," replied the sprightly girl, "we are used to winds and
snows here." Indeed they must be. On the mountains we found
snow, and the wind was piercing cold.

Before leaving this part of the country I must run back a little
to the town of Cumberland. The vicinity of this place is the
wildest I have yet seen. For about one mile the road is cut
through a mountain of rocks [The Narrows] and presents a
solemn and stupendous spectacle. Just from the side of the road
rocks rise on rocks to a height of perhaps 250 feet, thousands
and millions resting one on another, some with grey heads and
others with opaque frowns frowning down upon the traveller,
and to look up at them he feels as if they are almost ready to
tumble down upon and crush him to atoms. Here and there a
few stunted trees are seen growing out of the crevices and they
too seem to feel as if the hand of terror was upon them. Great
God! how manifold are thy works! Oh! who would not bow in
meek submission to Him who weigheth the mountains in scales
and the hills in a balance.

From Frostburg we rode 55 miles to Union[town] Pa. to
breakfast at 8 o'clock a.m. Sunday [the] 5th. From Union [to]
Washington 36 miles to dinner at ½ past 3 p.m. and I did ample
justice thereto both because I was very hungry and the dinner a
very good one. Among other things they had a kind of Cake
made of flour and was delightful. They give this to eat with
preserves and cream, not a little to moisten it with, but a
tumbler full. They offered me Coffee as usual, but poh, who
would drink Coffee when they could get cream. This is the
country for cream and butter and fine cows. How I longed to
have two or three of the latter which I saw on the road, safe in
my yard at home. Mary might milk them.

This Conestoga wagon, which actually carried freight on the old National Road, was photographed in 1906.

After dinner leaving Washington we reached Wheeling at 10 o'clock p.m. distance from Wash'n 32 miles. The distance therefore from Baltimore to Wheeling is 287 miles, 60 by rail road & 227 by stage. For the drivers on this route I can say that I found not one that was contrary or mulish, but polite and good and careful men. Few roads of the same distance but what would have some exception probably.

After getting supper at Wheeling I went to bed at 11 o'clock but did not sleep well having eaten too heartily. Wheeling contains about 10,000 inhabitants and is generally a very busy bustling place being a place of embarkation and landing of goods for the surrounding Country. It has but one street of any consequence, shut in by a mountain on one side and the Ohio river on the other.

Monday morning 6 April. It was a little rainy (a nice shower having fallen in the night) and very cold, but about 10 o'clock clouds began to break and grow fair, not however before having given us a smart sprinkle of hail.

After breakfast I went out to enquire about a Steam Boat [down the Ohio River to Cincinnati]. The only one at the wharf ready to go down was the Pensacola. I accordingly had my baggage on board, my berth taken and passage to Cincinnati paid, ready to be again moving. But I found here and subsequently that none of the boats on the Ohio are prompt, freight being their principle object they wait as long as they can and stop frequently at the intermediate ports. Finally, instead of 10, at 3½ p.m. we were ready to bid adieu to Wheeling. Whack, Whack—Whack Whack, phiz, phiz, phiz, hough hough, and the high pressure engines are at work, our boat begins to move, and off we slip at 15 knots to the hour.

A HIGHWAY OF COMMERCE

"I have stayed over night when there would be thirty six-horse teams in the wagon yard, one hundred Kentucky mules in an adjacent lot, one thousand hogs in other enclosures, and as many fat cattle from Illinois in adjoining fields."

On the road in its heyday, that was the scene recorded by one traveler at one wagon stand on one evening. The National Road was a highway of commerce. Before this, it took six to eight weeks for goods to be transported from Baltimore to the Ohio Valley; after completion of the National Road, sometimes as little as two weeks. With the increase in speed came a sharp increase in traffic. By one calculation, in 1822, Wheeling's six freight offices took deliveries from nearly 5,000 wagons—representing an estimated $400,000 in hauling charges paid out to the drivers.

Wagoners made extensive use of the Conestoga wagon, which, fitted for freight and pulled by six to twelve stalwart horses, could haul up to 10,000 pounds of goods. It was more practical to ship meat on the hoof. Although some was salted and sent by wagon, most of the beef, pork, and mutton reaching East Coast markets from the Midwest got there in droves of thousands of cattle, hogs, and sheep. Such droves were a common sight on the road, often announced from a distance by the massive clouds of dust they raised.

For practical reasons, wagoners and drovers had their own overnight stops separate and apart from the inns and taverns serving the stagecoaches and private conveyances. Necessity dictated large pens and pastures for the droves of animals, wagon yards for the horses and wagons, and barns for hay and grain, as well as accommodations for drivers and drovers.

* * *

Wagoners—or "pike boys," as they were often called—had some hard times and they had some good times, as wagoner John Deets recalled. He and Jesse Piersol plied the road during its busiest days as a highway of commerce.

John Deets

JOHN DEETS, The 1820s and 1830s
By Freight Wagon, Baltimore to Wheeling

My brother, Michael Deets, about four years older than myself, was among the first that wagoned on the pike. That was about the year 1822. He first drove his father's team, and the first load of goods he hauled from Baltimore was to Uniontown for Isaac Beeson or Isaac Skiles, I am not certain which. After that he drove for Abram Beagle, who lived in the west end of Uniontown. After that he bought a team, and a few years after bought two more, so that he owned three teams at one time. He drove one of the teams himself and hired drivers for the other two. The team he drove himself was a bell team.

The pike boys had some hard times and they had some good times. They were generally very fond of sport, and mostly tried to put up where the landlord was a fiddler, so that they could take a hoe-down. Every one carried his own bed, and after they had all the sport they wanted they put their beds down on the

A modernday near look-alike for John Deets: Ray Willford, at Truck City, a truckers' stop outside Frederick, Maryland. His successor to the Conestoga wagon has a gross weight of something like 76,000 pounds and is powered by a 365-horse Cummings diesel working through a nine-speed-plus-overdrive transmission.

floor in a circle, with their feet to the fire, and slept like a mouse in a mill. They were generally very sociable and friendly with each other, but I must note one thing just here: Two of the boys met at David Barnett's, some three miles east of Hancock, and got into a dispute, which was not often the case. Elias Meek and Abner Benley were the two. Meek was for fight, Benley was for peace. But Meek pushed on Benley and Benley run, but Meek caught him. Then Benley knew he had to fight, and turned on Meek and gave him a wonderful thrashing, so that he was not able to drive his team for some time.

And now with regard to getting up and down hills. They had no trouble to get up, but the trouble was in getting down, for they had no rubbers then, and to tight lock would soon wear out their tires. They would cut a small pole about 10 or 11 feet long and tie it to the bed with the lock chain and then bend it against the hind wheel and tie it to the feed through, or the hind part of the wagon bed, just tight enough to let the wheel turn slow. Sometimes one driver would wear out from 15 to 20 poles between Baltimore and Wheeling. Sometimes others would cut down a big tree and tie it to the hind end of the wagon and drop it at the foot of the hill. When there was ice, and there was much of it in winter, they had to use rough locks and cutters, and the wagon would sometimes be straight across the road, if not the hind end foremost. The snow was sometimes so deep that they had to go through fields, and shovel the drifts from the fences.... Those of us who had to go through the fields were three days going nine miles. This was in the neighborhood of Frostburg, Md. There were no bridges then across the Monongahela or the Ohio rivers. Wagoners had to ferry across in small flat-boats, and sometimes to lay at the rivers for some days, until the ice would run out or the river freeze over. A small bridge across Dunlap's creek, at Brownsville, broke down with one of the pike boys and did a great deal of damage. Sometimes a barrel of coffee would spring a leak and the coffee would be scattered along the road, and women would gather it up and be glad for such a prize. The writer has scattered some in his time.

JESSE J. PIERSOL, The 1840s and 1850s
By Freight Wagon, Cumberland to Wheeling

I have stayed over night with William Sheets [on Negro Mountain] when there would be thirty six-horse teams on the wagon yard,

"The Snow-Storm."

Strother, *Virginia Illustrated*

one hundred Kentucky mules in an adjacent lot, one thousand hogs in other enclosures, and as many fat cattle from Illinois in adjoining fields. The music made by this large number of hogs, in eating corn on a frosty night, I will never forget.

After supper and attention to the teams, the wagoners would gather in the bar room and listen to music on the violin, furnished by one of their fellows, have a "Virginia hoe-down," sing songs, tell anecdotes, and hear the experience of drivers and drovers from all points on the road, and when it was all over, unroll their beds, lay them down on the floor before the bar room fire, side by side, and sleep, with their feet near the fire, as soundly as under the paternal roof.

Coming out from Cumberland in the winter of 1851 or 1852, we stopped one night with Hiram Sutton, at Sand Springs, near Frostburg. The night was hazy, but not cold. We sat on our buckets, turned bottom up, and listened to a hundred horses grinding corn. One of our number got up in the night and complained that snow was falling on his face. This aroused us all, and we got up, went to the door and witnessed the most blinding snow storm I ever saw. Some of the horses broke loose from the tongue, and we had difficulty in finding them. We stayed up till morning, when the snow had risen to the hubs of the front wheels. We hitched eight or ten horses to a wagon, pulled out to Coonrod's tavern, one mile west, and returned to Sutton's for another wagon, and in this way all reached Coonrod's.

The next morning we pulled out again, and on little Savage mountain found the snow deeper than ever, and a gang of men engaged in shoveling it from the road. I got stuck and had to be shoveled out. We reached Tom Johnson's that night, making three miles in two days. The next day John Ullery, one of our number, upset at Peter Yeast's, and a barrel of Venetian Red [a reddish pigment] rolled out from his wagon, which painted the snow red for many miles, east and west. We stayed with Yeast the third night after the storm.

In the winter of 1848 a gang of us went down, loaded with tobacco, bacon, lard, cheese, flour, corn, oats and other products. One of our number was an Ohio man, named McBride. His team consisted of seven horses, the seventh being the leader. His load consisted of nine hogsheads of tobacco, five standing upright in the bed of his wagon, and four resting crosswise on top of the five. The hogsheads were each about four feet high and three and a half feet in diameter at the bulge and weighing from nine to eleven hundred pounds each. This made a "top-heavy load," and on the hill west of Somerfield, and near Tom Brown's tavern, the road icy, McBride's load tumbled over, the tobacco in the ditches, and the horses piled up in all shapes. The working of restoring the wreck was tedious, and before we got through with it we had the aid of thirty or forty wagoners not of our company. Of course the occasion brought to the ground a supply of the pure old whisky of that day, which was used in moderation and produced no bad effects. After we had righted our unfortunate fellow wagoner we pushed on and rested over night at Dan Augustine's, east of Petersburg.

In September, 1844 or 5, my father came home from Uniontown at night, and woke me up to tell me that there had been a big break in the Pennsylvania Canal, and that all western freights were coming over the National Road in wagons. The stage coaches brought out posters soliciting teams. By sunrise next morning, I was in Brownsville with my team, and loaded up at Cass's warehouse with tobacco, bacon, and wool, and whipped off for Cumberland. I drove to Hopwood with a load of flour from a back country mill. When we got beyond Laurel Hill, Snyder retailed his flour by the barrel to the tavern keepers, and was all sold out when we reached Coonrod's yard. Snyder told me to unhitch and feed, but leave the harness on. At midnight we rose, hitched up, Snyder lending me two horses, making me a team of eight, pulled out, and reached Cumberland that night. On leaving Coonrod's the night was dark, and I shall never forget the sounds of crunching stones under the wheels of my wagon, and the streaks of fire rolling out from the horses' feet.

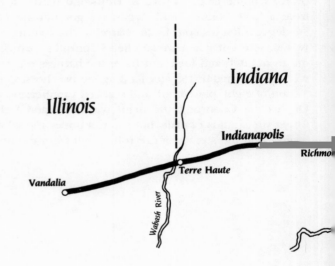

IV. FROM THE MOUNTAINS TO THE PRAIRIES

*Extension of the National Road
through Ohio, Indiana, and Illinois*

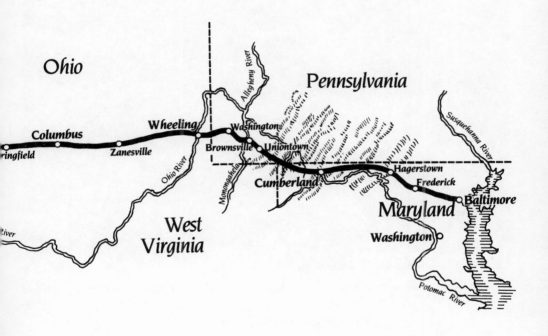

Washington Street, Indianapolis, 1825, the future route of the National Road.

THROUGH OHIO TO THE WEST

Doubtless in stentorian tones, a narrator read the Declaration of Independence, word for word. The Belmont County Light Cavalry responded with a volley of rifle fire; and then the speaker of the day—William B. Hubbard, later a state senator—followed with a prediction: that the great road would eventually go beyond just uniting Ohio with the East; someday it would stretch as far west as the Rocky Mountains.

The day was July 4, 1825, and they were gathered in front of the Belmont County Courthouse in St. Clairsville, Ohio, to break ground for the long-awaited National Road west of Wheeling. Four months earlier, virtually to the day, Congress had finally made the western extension a certainty with a key appropriation of $150,000.

It was an auspicious moment. As if to make it even more auspicious, Secretary of War James Barbour—whose Army Corps of Engineers now had responsibility for construction and maintenance of the entire road—announced that this new section, as far as Zanesville, would be built using the most modern method of road construction in the world: a new technology devised only a few years earlier by the Scotsman John L. McAdam.

Though well engineered for its day, the road already built through Maryland, Pennsylvania, and Virginia had not held up under the unexpectedly heavy pounding of traffic. The sand and gravel surface was no match for 10-ton wagons and swiftly flying coaches and droves of fatted cattle. The new method of road building, soon to be known as macadam, had so far been tried only once in the United States: three years earlier on a section of the privately built National Pike, between Boonsboro and Hagerstown in Maryland, where it gave great promise.

This early macadam consisted of three strata of crushed stone, roughly 15 inches deep at the center, and differed from the construction of the National Road between Cumberland and Wheeling in the use of much more finely crushed stone and the rolling and compacting of the stone between layers. This made for a packed surface, the particles of stone and dust combining with moisture to form a kind of cement. (Later macadam also involved the application of a binder as part of the compacting process—at first water, and then a bitumen—so that the original form of the pavement had a somewhat different appearance from that of modern macadam.) The westward extension, with a cleared width of 80 feet, was also wider.

Construction of the road in Ohio had been long awaited, amid nagging doubts of its ever becoming a reality. The National Road had reached Wheeling in 1818 and stopped. In 1820, Congress did appropriate $10,000 to survey the road as far as the Mississippi, but nothing was to be seen except a few surveyor's stakes. Meanwhile, Indiana (1816) and Illinois (1818) had become states and also had compacts with the federal government for extending the National Road through to their capitals, Indianapolis and Vandalia. Ohio itself had built a road from Wheeling west to Zanesville in 1804, but it was wholly inadequate compared with the federally built road east of Wheeling; it was only 20 feet wide, and to expedite construction the contracts had allowed for leaving stumps up to a foot high in the roadway. Equally inadequate was Zane's Trace, linking Wheeling (then Zanesburg) with Maysville, Kentucky, by way of Zanesville, and laid out by Ebenezer Zane in accordance with a 1796 federal grant of property in Ohio, the condition being that he blaze a trail along that route.

By comparison, the new National Road to Zanesville, when completed along a new alignment, must have seemed one of the best roads in the world, and probably was. And almost from the start, the new road did big business. According to an official report, traffic through Zanesville during 1832 included 2,357 wagons with three or more horses, 11,613 two-horse carriages and wagons, 14,907 one-horse carriages, and 35,310 riders on horseback, as well as 16,750 horses and mules, 24,410 sheep, 52,845 hogs, and 96,323 cattle, all in droves.

At much its usual speed, the National Road crept west—to Columbus in 1833, to Springfield in 1838. The stretch between Zanesville and Columbus, according to a report by National Road Commissioner Jonathan Knight, was only one mile longer overall than if it had followed a practically impossible, absolutely straight line; and it had no grade greater than 3 degrees except

Washington Street today: an urban canyon.

Four distinctive types of milestones typical of separate sections of the National Road can still be found: A) along the old Baltimore National Pike (near Hancock, Maryland, showing 95 miles to Baltimore); B) the Cumberland Road (just outside Cumberland, Maryland); C) the extension of the National Road into Ohio (Brookside); and D) the National road in Indiana (near Centerville). The latter shows nine miles to the Ohio state line, 4½ miles to Richmond, and one mile to Centerville).

Among the first tollhouses on the National Road was this one in LaVale, Maryland, six miles west of Cumberland, shown here as it appeared in an illustration in *Harper's Magazine,* November 1879, and as it is today. It was built about 1833.

Among the last of the tollhouses—shown here abandoned, about 1890—was this one on East Washington Street, Indianapolis, near what is now Shadeland Avenue.

Courtesy of the Indiana Historical Society

for a particularly hilly section near Zanesville. Elsewhere in Ohio, the road was nearly as straight and level.

Meanwhile, surveying, clearing of right of way, and in some cases grading and paving continued westward through Ohio. Work on the Indiana section of the road began in Indianapolis in 1827, reaching out both east and west simultaneously. But with the exception of macadamizing the road through the state capital, the federal government never went beyond the clearing of right of way. The state was left to complete the job, which it did in 1850. In Illinois, work began in 1830 and was completed by the federal government to Vandalia in 1839; but the road was only clay-surfaced.

The reason for a decline and then halt in federal participation was a major change in the road's status: section by section, it was becoming state-owned, albeit still with the name of "National Road." Congress had considered converting it to a toll road several times in the 1820s, only to hold back on Constitutional grounds. Since the major share of appropriations for the road was going into new construction, maintenance of the completed sections suffered increasingly with each passing year. Almost a decade after Postmaster General Meigs's inspection tour, the road was still largely as he had found it. Meanwhile, an intensification of sectional rivalries was putting a continually tighter squeeze on the federal funds available to the National Road. Other sections of the country had begun demanding their own national roads. And about this same time, a new president took office. John Quincy Adams had been a loose constructionist of the internal-improvement provisions of the Constitution and thus a ready friend to the National Road; now his successor in 1829, Andrew Jackson, though a frequent traveler of the National Road, had come to office as "the people's candidate," pledging in his first annual message "construction of highways in the several States" (as opposed to one national road).

Although new construction was allowed to continue in the west as planned, the federal government began to divest itself of the National Road by turning it over to the respective states, which, being under no Constitutional constraints, were free to make it a toll road and use the revenues for its maintenance. Transfer began with Ohio in 1831 and continued with Pennsylvania and Maryland in 1832 and Virginia in 1833. In Indiana and Illinois, where the road was still under construction, federal ownership continued for the time being.

Prior to turning the Cumberland-to-Wheeling section of the road over to the states, however, the federal government agreed first to put it into respectable shape, rebuilding and macadamizing it where necessary. Ideally, this meant the whole road, for the local superintendent of the Army Corps of Engineers wrote to the chief engineer in Washington that he found the road "in a shocking condition...some of it impassable." The corps directed that the repairs go so far as removing the old stones in the road, raking the bed flat, and then rebuilding with layers of new, more finely broken stone, compacted in between, as had been done west of Wheeling. Much of the road was accordingly rebuilt, although not every mile. It was in 1832, also, that the Corps of Engineers undertook the largest single project on the road—the rerouting of the road at Cumberland. The original road had followed the approximate route of Braddock's Road over Haystack Mountain to the west, but it proved too steep for the wagons and coaches that were now the major part of the road's traffic. So the road was rerouted through The Narrows, a longer but considerably flatter route.

Almost as soon as transfer legislation had passed, Ohio authorized erection of toll gates at intervals of every 20 miles, or at least one to a county. At each, there was a massive gate of wrought iron or wood to be opened on payment of toll. Pennsylvania erected six toll houses within its 70-mile section; Maryland and Virginia likewise made their sections toll roads. Tolls varied from state to state, and according to what passed by—so much for a score of sheep or cattle, so much for a horse and rider, so much for a wagon. Since it was the wheels of the most heavily loaded wagons that were doing the greatest damage to the road surface, the toll schedule encouraged wider wheels through a descending scale of tolls, some schedules actually allowing free travel for any wagon with wheels 8 inches wide or wider.

Transfer of the National Road by the federal government was completed with the passage of legislation relinquishing the road in Indiana in 1848 and in Illinois eight years later. By then, however, the federal government had long since given up anything but nominal authority over the remaining sections of the road. Two decades earlier, in 1838, Congress had made its final National Road appropriation, bringing to $6,824,919.33 the total of federal expenditures in this great experiment in road building. And never since then has the federal government built a public highway; it has left road building to the states and localities—albeit with the help of federal appropriations astronomically larger than its entire investment in the National Road.

*   *   *

But as of the 1830s: Leaping the Alleghenies and now reaching the heartland of America, a road called "national" was just that.

A peculiarity of the National Road west of the Ohio River was the "S"-bridge, so called because of its shape. Where the road crossed a stream obliquely, the early engineers found it more difficult and more expensive to construct a bridge than where it crossed perpendicularly; so they made the crossing itself perpendicular and curved the bridge around and back in the shape of an "S." This one, built in 1830, is just west of New Concord, Ohio.

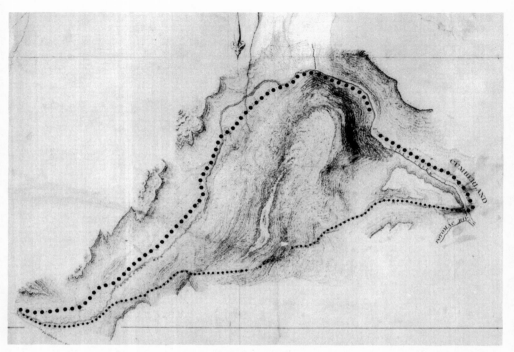

Prior to turning the National Road over to the states for administration and maintenance, the U.S. Army Corps of Engineers—the federal agency then with jurisdiction over the road—made several improvements, notably the macadamizing of especially bad sections. The Corps also changed the route of the road just west of Cumberland. The original Cumberland Road, using the old Indian trail and Braddock's route over Haystack Mountain (small dots), was too steep for the wagons and coaches that were now the major part of the road's traffic. So the road was rerouted through The Narrows, a longer but considerably flatter route (large dots). This also entailed construction of a bridge over Wills Creek. Above is the map prepared by the Corps of Engineers in 1832 in planning the project. Width of map detail is roughly five miles.

Cartographic and Architectural Branch, National Archives

The National Road bridge over Wills Creek at The Narrows (1833),
traversed about 1910 by horse and buggy. It was replaced by a
modern span in 1932.

U.S. Bureau of Public Roads (National Archives)

*Even if paved in primitive macadam here and clay there, even if
fully completed a hundred miles at a stretch only to become
little more than a clearing marked by surveyors' poles, it was a
road . . . a road now at least passable, a road west, the road by
which most of America's pioneer settlers went west.*

*Yet not all whose traveled it west of the Alleghenies, especial-
ly in its earlier years, were bound for distant climes. Indiana and
Illinois were still known as the West, and Ohio was still the
Frontier. Among those who went there by the National Road
were: William Faux, a gentleman farmer from England on a tour
through much of "the known West"; Robert Owen, the British
social reformer who sought to establish a model social community in New Harmony, Indiana, and used the National Road on
his way there, a journey recounted by his son William; Mary
Reed Eastman and her husband, Ornan, an ordained evangelist
and agent for the American Tract Society, recently appointed its
agent for the Mississippi Valley, on a journey they began one
month after their wedding; Edmund Flagg, a journalist from
Maine who moved to Kentucky, originally writing about his
travels for the Louisville Journal; and J. Richard Beste, who by
Conestoga wagon traveled with his wife and eleven children
like "the Swiss family Robinson Crusoes," on a journey that was
to have taken them to the Mississippi River but was cut short by
the hard realities of wagon travel on the frontier.*

WILLIAM FAUX, 1819
By Mail Coach, Hagerstown to Zanesville

Sunday, October 3rd. [1819]
We supped and slept at Hager's-town, a market town, with three
Dutch gothic churches, adorned with tall spires, and a good
court house. This town is highly delightful, and almost surrounded
by small mountains; the scenery is beautiful, and both in and
around an air of grandeur prevails; except, indeed, at our
tavern, where, though it is Sunday, all is smoke and fire, and
Bacchus is the god.

4th.
Early this morning we commenced a perilous journey, ascending and descending the Allegany mountains all day. All here is
wild, awfully precipitous, and darkly umbrageous, high as the
heavens, or low as perdition. I almost resolved on not returning
this way by mail [coach], which carries and keeps one in
constant alarm, unless the traveller has nerves of iron or brass.

Such, however, is the expertness of the drivers here, that there is no ground for real apprehension.

5th.

We rode this day over our English General Braddock's grave [actually re-interred in 1804]. To prevent the Indians in pursuit from discovering his body, he ordered it to be buried in the midst of the road, at the foot of the Allegany mountains in 1756 [1755].

I slept at [Brownsville], on the Monongahela, where are the remains of a British fort once used against the Indians.

6th.

Within two miles east of Washington, Pennsylvania, we found that the strap, which confined our luggage, had given way, and scattered Morgan's trunks and money a few miles behind. [Morgan was a fellow passenger traveling west with six Negro slaves.] We sent men and horses back, and to our surprise found all safe. On leaving Washington, several other gentlemen entered our stage, but would not permit Mr. Morgan and his negroes to enter.—"What?" said they, "ride with negroes?"—Much strife now ensued, and a battle was intended; but to quiet the angry passions of both sides, a stage was provided for the refusing party. Our ride, for the last three hours of our journey, was fearfully romantic, amongst huge rocks which hung over on both sides and seemed ready to fall upon us, the effect of which was greatly heightened by the moon-light.

Between twelve and one o'clock [a.m.] we reached Wheeling, Virginia, on the Ohio, and went supperless to bed. I shared mine with a young student, Mr. Paul, of Washington Academy, now bound to his father's house at Maddison Ville, Indiana, who is there a Banker, or Bank Director.

7th.

We found the Ohio river nearly dry, so droughty has been the summer. It is now fed only by mountain springs.

9th.

A miserably wet (and as sailors say) dirty day. I fell sick of Wheeling, imprisoned by a high and almost inaccessible mountain, to the top of which I climbed yesterday.

Sunday, 10th.

By free and frequent conversations with intelligent residents and travellers here, I find that public opinion is favourable to location in the western country, which they say has never yet lacked a market for surplus produce; and as men of capital only can raise produce, and as their number is comparatively few, it is unlikely that the surplus produce will ever greatly exceed the demand. Much of what is raised will necessarily be consumed by those who raise none; and some will always be wanted at New Orleans and other river towns, cities, and new settlements.

11th.

Waggons (not many) are daily arriving with goods and emigrants for the river, down which, when the waters rise, they are to float in flat boats called arks, two and two of many living creeping things, occasionally anchoring on the banks and surveying the promised land. A gentlemen recently called at the Cincinnati bank for specie, or good negotiable paper. "No," was the answer, "we, sir, have neither." The paper of that city, the pride of the west, is negotiable only in the city for necessaries, and there only at 30 and 40 per centum below par, or United States' paper. The best mode of dealing here is, on your arrival, to go to the Cincinnati broker and sell just so much of the United States' paper as will get you enough of their paper for expenses at the tavern or elsewhere; all must be spent here, none taken away, for out of the city it is mere waste paper. Such are banks, banking, and bankers; let therefore the traveller hereafter not depend on them, but take with him either hard dollars or notes of the United States' bank or its branches.

12th.

I left Wheeling at eight this morning; the tavern bill three and a half dollars per week for board merely. I crossed the Ohio into the state so called, and passed briskly through St. Clair's Ville and Morris-town, and a hilly country; all fine land in grain, corn, and pasture, with a beautiful clover face, white as with a shower of sleet; and abundance of flourishing orchards full, above and below, of excellent fruit, although sixteen years ago all was wild, and a complete forest. In almost every orchard is seen a cider press, and under every tree large apples, so thick that at every step you must tread upon them, while the boughs above are breaking down with their overladen weight. It is here no crime for either man or beast to rob orchards. Land is worth from 15 to 30 dollars an acre, with all improvements included, and a market, as yet, for all surplus produce. At 30 miles' end, I rested for the night at a homely but comfortable stage-house on the road, with a young Irishman, Robert G. Ormsby, Esq. of Louisville, Kentucky, aged 21, of fine person and manners, and a fellow student of the celebrated Irish orator, Charles Phillips, Esq.

13th.

I started alone at three this morning, well pleased with Mr. Ormsby, who mounted his stage for the east, and I mine for the west. In consequence of thus meeting with this gentleman, I determined for the future, on always breaking through the custom of waiting for introductions before entering into conversation.

At four this morning, on the driver getting down to lock the wheel, the horses started, and instantly struck a stump of a tree, and upset the mail[coach] with a crashing fall, which bruised my side, cut my face, and blackened my eyes; the two leaders [lead horses] escaped into the forest, and we saw them no more. The driver went in pursuit of them, and left me to guard and sleep one hour and a half in the damaged vehicle, now nearly bottom upwards. When I awoke it was daylight, and I walked up to a farm log-house, the people of which put their heads out of the window and thus addressed me,—"Stranger, come *into* the fire!" and I went in, without being burned. At five, the driver returned, and with two horses only, we got under weigh, and moved on through Cambridge and Washington to breakfast, and at sun-set reached our inn at Zainsville, where I determined on resting a few days to repair the damages of the past day.

My inn is a good one, stored with newspapers, and full of good things, and visitors to devour them; and the town of Zainsville is very flourishing, and likely to become a city. It is now a county seat and a fountain of law and justice, situated on the banks of the fair Muskingham river, 84 miles from Wheeling; eighteen years old, with 3,000 inhabitants; good land 20 dollars an acre; plenty of coal and excellent water, being well supplied by springs and the river, and affording good society; many strangers continually passing to and fro. Here is kept a folio register, in which travellers write their names, from whence they come, and whither they are bound, with any news which they bring with them.

WILLIAM OWEN, 1824
By Hired Hack and Stagecoach, Frederick to Brownsville

[Robert Owen and his son William, along with Donald Macdonald and Stedman Whitwell, "two prospective communal companions," set out from New York for New Harmony in mid-November 1824, traveling by boat to Baltimore and thence by

Robert Owen, social reformer, father of William.

stage to Washington, where Robert Owen met with and described his plans to Secretary of State John Quincy Adams and Secretary of War John C. Calhoun. The actual trip west began on November 28. Missing the 4:00 a.m. stagecoach, they sought out hack drivers on the streets of Washington until they found two of them willing to take the group to Hagerstown by horse-drawn hack (at $6 a day for a trip of two days each way). At Hagerstown, the group caught a stage to Brownsville, thence a steamboat down the Ohio to Evansville, Indiana, whence they made their way to New Harmony. William Owen's narrative begins here as they approach Frederick in their hired hacks.]

Monday, 29th November

We started by daybreak about half past 5 and went to Fredericktown, 15 miles to breakfast, over a very rough and hilly road, through a romantic country, where we arrived about half past 11. On the road I discovered that I had left my watch behind. I therefore wrote a note at Fredericktown to Mrs. Shelley [at whose inn in Clarksburg, Maryland they had stayed the night of leaving Washington], requesting her that it might be sent to Godby's Hotel, Washington. We stopped at Talbott's who gave us a good breakfast. While there several droves of hogs passed: they were proceeding to Baltimore, coming from Ohio and Kentucky. The morning was wet and during the greater part of the day, the fog continued to hide the prospect from us. We started about 1 o'clock and arrived between seven and eight at Boonsboro, 15 miles distant, having crossed the South mountain, the first of the range of Blue mountains. We passed thro a romantic hilly country in which lay some fine farms. I particularly remarked a little village beautifully situated in a small cultivated valley, surrounded by finely wooded hills, which reminded me much of Swiss scenery.

Capt. McDonald, Hunter [otherwise unidentified] and I who were together in one carriage, had a very interesting conversation regarding the Indians, and past recollections, and future anticipations, more particularly regarding a new state of society.

We supped at the Hotel at Boonsboro, which appeared to be very comfortable. One of our horses was knocked up, but having obtained another, we proceeded 12 miles further to Hagerstown, on the Antietam creek. We traveled in the dark and arrived about 11 o'clock. We went to the Stage Office, where we found a host rather nonchalant. We were told that we could have no other conveyance than the stage which should start next morning at 4 o'clock. Tho' a great deal fatigued, it was determined to go on by it in order to cross the mountains as long as we had fine weather.

Tuesday, 30 November

Having been awoke at half past three, we started at four and proceeded 27 miles to Hancocktown to breakfast. We arrived about half past 10 and found that they had give us up for the day. We however soon got a good breakfast. Hancock is a small village prettily situated. On starting we had an excellent driver who carried us on fast. We passed through a most romantic country, continually ascending and descending hills, one, two and three miles in height, which gave us a varied prospect of hills and dales partly cultivated but mostly wooded with oak, interspread with black and white hickory, black and white walnut, the tulip tree, sycamore, etc. Several mountain tops are covered with white pines, but of course, forests are at present bare, only the faded oak leaves still left here and there to point out what is wanting to the scene.

We met on the road the proprietor of the stage, who drove us the following stage, partly with six horses. We supped at 6 at Slicers and arrived at Cumberland at ½ p. 10 [10:30], very much tired, indeed. This day we crossed Sidling hill and Tower hill, which is 112 miles from Baltimore, and afterwards Nicholas mount. These mountains are part of the chain of the Allegheny's which separate the Mississippi rivers from the east coast. On the road between Fredericktown and Washington, Pa., we met continually droves of hogs, often 600 together, being driven, usually from Ohio and even Indiana, to Baltimore. They traveled 8 and 10 miles a day and of course must repay the expenses of even such a journey or no one would undertake it.

An old engraving titled "En Route."

Strother, *Virginia Illustrated*

We also passed and over took a great number of wagons with 4, 5, or 6 horses always in good condition and high spirits, of good breed and well fed. Got to bed about ½ p. 11. A most delightful day. We walked up several hills, but found the weather rather too hot for such exercise. The stage is a long body on springs and can contain 14 persons on the inside. It has a wooden covering and back and leather sides. These we found it very pleasant to have rolled up on both sides in the day, during the whole journey. Fine clear moonlight.

Wednesday, 1st Dec.

Started per stage, as being the only conveyance, at ½ p. 5. We went 14 miles to breakfast and arrived about ½ p. 10 at Allegheny, having crossed the Savage Mount. The whole of the scenery was very romantic and beautiful, especially from the tops of the heights to which we ascended. The view was fine, alternate hill and dale, often enlivened by clear meandering streams and by large cleared and fertile tracts of land or sometimes by neat little villages, one of which in particular reminded me of Swiss scenery, being composed of rustic log houses with rough wooded roofs, lying in a finely wooded valley in the Blue Mountains. We proceeded from Allegheny with 6 horses, to a beautiful valley in Pa., in which lies Smithfield, a nice little village whose situation struck me more than any I had yet seen. Here we met General Jackson, who had just arrived. He is a fine looking old man and widower. We overtook several parties of emigrants, all bound for the Ohio. They had usually a wagon with their utensils, and often a horse or two for some of the party to ride. They traveled 18 or 20 miles per day. The greater part of the road was encompassed by trees and from the top of the different ridges of the Allegheny's which we traversed this day we had wide extended prospects, less romantic than those of the Blue Mountains. We were advised to proceed- immediately. We therefore this time supped and started, because' an hour's sleep would make us swear when awoke, the host said. We reached Brownsville about ½ p. 4 and were told we must wait for daylight. We laid down on the floor, feet to the fire, and slept till 6, when we breakfasted and proceeded at 7 to cross the Monongahela river in a ferry. We passed a finely undulated country and reached Washington, Pa. at 2 o'clock. The day had been cloudy and now it commenced raining pretty smartly. On the road we never got washed till we stopped for breakfast and then we had no conveniences for it. We now got dressed and washed, and while we were undressed and thus employed, a stage arrived. The parties were shown into the same room as we possessed. A young lady, daughter of a

General and Senator (Beecher) came in while we were thus employed, and with great nonchalance sat by the fire and dressed her hair. We dined and slept till 9, supped and went to bed.

Friday, 3rd Dec.
Started at 5 per mail [coach] for Pittsburg. It rained pretty heavily, though it ceased after some time. The road, as we now left the National turnpike, was very hilly.

[Robert Owen visited briefly in Pittsburgh with George Rapp, the social and religious leader from whom he bought his Indiana settlement. The group then proceeded down the Ohio by steamboat to Louisville and thence, by way of Evansville, to the former Rappite settlement of Harmony that Owen called New Harmony.]

MARY REED EASTMAN, 1833
By Stagecoach, Near Zanesville to Frederick

Mary Reed Eastman in later years.

Courtesy of The Schlesinger Library, Radcliffe College

[Mary, age 26, of Marblehead, Massachusetts and Ornan Eastman, an evangelist and agent for the American Tract Society, had been married less than a month when they left Massachusetts November 5, 1832 on a trip to the Mississippi Valley on behalf of the Tract Society. Going by way of New York, Savannah, and New Orleans, they traveled by steamship, stagecoach, open wagon, and occasionally railroad, and logged a total of 5,435 miles before arriving back in New York, headquarters of the Tract Society, on July 4, 1833. The return trip took them along part of the National Road.]

Zanesville, Ohio. On the Muskingum. Wednesday, June 26
One day nearer home! I have not before been able to realize that we were indeed going home, but it really appears like it now; & if we do not stop at Pittsburg, we shall be but a few days more on our journey. We have heard that the cholera prevails at P. [Pittsburgh] & if it proves to be the case, we shall proceed directly to Philadelphia.

We left Columbus yesterday at noon. The road [apparently not the National] was very bad—a great deal of rain had fallen in 3 days, & the mud was very deep. There was a great deal of the railroad [that is, wood rails placed across the road], & it was often broken through. We were tossed about most unmercifully, & an imaginative mind would have thought itself sometimes nearer the sky than the earth. There is nothing more calculated to keep one's eyes open, & learn to take care of one's self and stand on our own feet, than such a ride. There was only one man beside ourselves in the stage, and we had full scope for our limbs to play. No need of Calisthenics then; but great danger if one's mouth is open, of such a jar as would break a tooth or bite the tongue. We were comforted in believing we had a strong stage & good drivers.

After we left Granville [near Newark, east of Columbus and north of the route of the National Road], the road was better & 12 miles farther, we came on the Great National Road, or "the Pike," as the people call it here [the new macadamized section from Wheeling west], which was very smooth & good, & we slept sweetly, undisturbed, until we reached Zanesville soon after 12. We hesitated about going farther, & should have had the stage to ourselves, but we were quite fatigued & having so recently recovered from indisposition, judged it most prudent to stop for one day at least, for there is no place we should be willing to remain in, nearer than 100 miles. There has been so much of cholera in Wheeling & the vicinity, it will be best only to pass through the town. An Episcopal clergyman & his wife have just left this tavern in a private carriage for Lexington— inquired of us about Bishop Smith. They were thrown down a bank 16 ft high, 2 days since, but wonderfully escaped any serious injury. Poor creatures, they will have to endure some rough roads [going west] & many heavy jars, before they reach their journey's end—for they have had the best of the travelling. I hope we have gone through all the troughs & deeps & shall find our way smooth as we proceed. We certainly have had a full share of hard rubbing, & if we get over the Mountains safely, I hope we shall be rubbed bright at last.

A most delightful day this—& I am enjoying the comfort of a room in a public house, where no one cares for me, or troubles me with "polite attentions," except to give what I ask for. It is a luxury sometimes to feel alone.

Frederick, Maryland. Saturday 29 June
We took the stage at Zanesville on Wednesday night at 11 o'clock. The road was smooth & excellent, so that we could sleep very quietly, the morning was delightful, the air clear & cool, & the country through which we passed was rich & varied in scenery, though the fields of corn & grain were not as forward as those we saw a week before between Cincinnati & Columbus. I wondered not, that so many told us "it would be very pretty riding on the Pike"—It has been Mc'Adamized & is now perfectly smooth, the hills have been so nearly levelled, that the horses can trot up with the greatest ease, & there is no

need of locking the wheels in descending. The bridges over the numerous creeks are all of stone, & very handsome as well as durable. There is no road in the United States equal to this, extending more than 100 miles, in such perfect order. We reached Wheeling on Thursday at 12 not much fatigued; heard the cholera was in Pittsburg, & the people generally alarmed there, so that there appeared no prospect of Mr. E[astman]'s accomplishing anything, if he should attempt it; for the people are not in a state to listen to any public object. Therefore, we concluded to go directly to Baltimore & proposed to go as far as Washington 32 miles, & stop for the night. The Mail Stage was going with no other passengers, & if we would go in that & travel all night and the next day, until we overtook the Accommodation [stagecoach] at Cumberland, we were offered the privilege of resting that night, taking that stage next morn as far as we pleased, & then to enter the Mail again if we preferred.

The Stage was a very comfortable one, & the weather so pleasant, we concluded to go; & at 3 o'clock left Wheeling, which is a small place & very dirty from the quantities of coal dust, which fill the town in every direction. Although we were still on the National Road, it was not so good as in Ohio. It has been made many years & was originally formed of large stones; spaces between which, were filled with sandstone, but this is now worn off & the earth around them washed away & we were constantly riding over large rough rocks. The night was pleasant, & we slept part of the time. At daylight, we crossed the Monongahela at Brownsville in a flat boat, which was "poled across".

About 6 miles before we reached the breakfast house, a gentleman & lady joined us, who were in a stage that broke down the evening before; and soon we began to ascend the Mountains. At the foot of Laurel Hill, 2 more horses were attached to our team, on one of which sat a little boy to guide us & then we went up, & up & up 3 miles, admiring the hills and forests around & the prospects which were ever varying. There were a great many chestnut trees covered with blooms, around the sides of the hills, which were quite ornamental—& the varieties of laurels (among which, the Mountain laurel or Rhododendron) were abundant on each side of us. The vast mass of forest trees around, above & below us, & afar off in every direction as far as the eye could reach, surpassed in beauty anything I had ever seen.

From the top of Laurel Hill, we had a view of Union Town, which we had left 6 miles distant. The collection of dwelling houses, the fields cultivated with grain of different kinds, and all distinctly visible by their several colors, formed a most beautiful picture. Would that I could describe all I saw. My brain almost aches from the variety of images that fill it, which words cannot describe. But we went up & down from morn till night, seeing and admiring something new at every turn. The road was generally good. Many were employed breaking stones to cover it, or repair it, where it was worn—but when we descended, the horses trotted every step as fast as they could go. At noon it rained, but the sun shone again before 5, & the prospect was more beautiful from the contrast. At one point, our driver told us we had risen to an elevation of 1400 ft, during 5 miles, & it really seemed as if we were far above all the rest of the world, seeing nothing above us but the sky, & the mountains far below us, completely encircling us. The clouds that sometimes rested on the sides of the distant mountains, seemed like rivers separating them, so beautiful & white. Even on these elevated spots were to be seen flourishing villages & well cultivated fields, so that we were still "in, although above the world."

But such an elevated station we could not long occupy, but must descend to the vales below; & now the road became rough, & at one time for 5 miles we were continually on the descent, with the exception of a level of ⅛ of a mile. The horses appeared to fly & we were but just able to keep our seats, while in such rapid motion. The lady with us could not keep still, but would bound from side to side with such force, her husband was obliged to hold her with all his strength; but we reached Cumberland with no other accident, than breaking the iron of the wheel. Here we meant to pass the night, but having rode a few miles in the Accommodation, & seeing the horses & drivers far inferior to those in the Mail, & fearing we should drag along a whole day, to gain the distance we might otherwise reach in half that time; & *moreover,* both of us being actually better & not as much fatigued as on the first day, we concluded to proceed on the journey. We were again alone in a very comfortable coach & slept quietly, occasionally waking to admire the enchanting scene. What could be more romantic than to be on the Alleghanies in a fine moonlight night? The view was indeed sublime. All around us was clear & bright, while the fog rested on the country below us & appeared like the ocean, while here & there some of the highest peaks would tower above it, like distant islands. On one side of us were towering trees; and on the other, a valley in which the tops of the trees just reached us, & the white clouds of fog lying on them made us feel as if we were on the brink of a precipice, with the ocean at our feet. At sunrise too, the scene was beautiful & here others were added to our party. We breakfasted at Hagerstown, a pretty place, & reached Frederick at 12 noon,

"The road was generally good. Many were employed breaking stones to cover it, or repair it, where it was worn."—Mary Reed Eastman

Road repair work near Farmington, Pennsylvania. The "flagman" is Carol Dorsey of Graysville.

after riding 300 miles, without stopping, & much less fatigued than we should have believed possible, had we calculated to come rapidly.

Mr. E. called on Rev. Mr. Smith, but did not see him, & after tea the gentleman came with his wife to see us; regretted their family was so situated, they could not invite us to remain with them. But we are very well accommodated at the Hotel & after so much jolting & tossing, it is a comfort to be alone, where I can rest as much as I please & do as I wish. & here we are on the Eastern side of the Alleghanies. It seems like a dream that I have passed over so great an extent of country in so short a time, & seen so much that is beautiful & grand. But is it too true for a dream.

[According to a log in Mary Eastman's diary, the trip from Columbus to Frederick, totaling 362 miles, was made in 61 hours. At six miles per hour, that was not a remarkable speed per hour but it was a remarkable elapsed time for traveling 362 miles. On Monday, July 1st, the Eastmans left Frederick, taking the new Baltimore & Ohio Railroad to Baltimore; and from there completed the journey to New York by steamboat and canal boat.]

EDMUND FLAGG, 1836
On Horseback, Vandalia and Vicinity

[Summer]
With the situation and appearance of Vandalia I was not, as I have expressed myself, much prepossessed; indeed, I was somewhat disappointed. Though not prepared for anything very striking, yet in the capital of a state we always anticipate something, if not superior or equal, at least not inferior to neighbouring towns of less note. Its site is an elevated, undulating tract upon the west bank of the Kaskaskia, and was once heavily timbered, as are now it suburbs. The streets are of liberal breadth—some of them not less than eighty feet from kerb to kerb—enclosing an elevated public square nearly in the centre of the village, which a little expenditure of time and money might render a delightful promenade. The public edifices are very inconsiderable, consisting of an ordinary structure of brick for legislative purposes; a similar building originally erected as a banking establishment, but now occupied by the offices of the state authorities; a Presbyterian Church, with

cupola and bell, besides a number of lesser buildings for purposes of worship and education.

Here also is a land-office for the district, and the Cumberland Road is permanently located and partially constructed to the place. An historical and antiquarian society has here existed for about ten years, and its published proceedings evince much research and information. "The Illinois Magazine" was the name of an ably-conducted periodical commenced at this town some years since, and prosperously carried out by Judge [James] Hall [see above], but subsequently removed to Cincinnati. Some of the articles published in this magazine, descriptive of the state, were of high merit. It is passing strange that a town like Vandalia, with all the natural and artificial advantages it possesses; located nearly twenty years ago, by state authority, expressly as the seat of government; situated upon the banks of a fine stream, which small expense would render navigable for steamers, and in the heart of a healthy and fertile region, should have increased and flourished no more than seems to have been the case. Vandalia will continue the seat of government until the year 1840; when, agreeable to the late act of Legislature, it is to be removed to Springfield, where an appropriation of $50,000 has been made for a state-house now in progress.

The growth of Vandalia, though tardy, can perhaps be deemed so only in comparison with the more rapid advancement of neighbouring towns; for a few years after it was laid off it was unsurpassed in improvement by any other. We are told that the first legislators who assembled in session at this place sought their way through the neighbouring prairies as the mariner steers over the trackless ocean, by his knowledge of the cardinal points. Judges and lawyers came pouring in from opposite directions, as wandering tribes assemble to council; and many were the tales of adventure and mishap related at their meeting. Some had been lost in the prairies; some had slept in the woods; some had been almost chilled to death, plunging through creeks and rivers.

I pursued my route along the great national road [in the direction of] Terre Haute. This road is projected eighty feet in breadth, with a central carriage-path of thirty feet, elevated above all standing water, and in no instance to exceed three degrees from a perfect level. The work has been commenced along the whole line, and is under various stages of advancement; for most of the way, it is perfectly direct. The bridges are to be of limestone, and of massive structure, the base of the abutments being equal in depth to one third their altitude. The work was for a while suspended, for the purpose of investigating former operations, and subsequently through failure of an appropriation from Congress; but a grant has since been voted sufficient to complete the undertaking so far as it is now projected. West of Vandalia the route is not yet located, though repeated surveys with reference to this object have been made. St. Louis, Alton, Beardstown, and divers other places upon the Mississippi and its branches present claims to become the favoured point of its destination. Upon this road I journeyed some miles; and, even in its present unfinished condition, it gives evidence of its enormous character. Compare this grand national work with the crumbling relics of the mound-builders scattered over the land, and remark the contrast: yet how, think you, reader, would an hundred thousand men regard an undertaking like this?

J. RICHARD BESTE, 1851
With the help of daughters LOUISE and LUCY BESTE
By Conestoga Wagon, Indianapolis to Terre Haute

My situation at Indianapolis, I found to be helpless. I had come by steamboat and railway as far as railway or steamboat could forward me in this direction. Water there was no more of; and the railways were completed no further. It was true that several lines were planned out, which would go to St. Louis and the Pacific: but we had no wish to stay at Indianapolis until they should be completed. I had been told that the stagecoach, direct from Cincinnati, passed through the town and along the National Road to the Mississippi: and to this I had trusted.

The stage coach came rolling up the street. I will not describe what has been described so often: suffice it to say that it held places for three with their backs to the horses; and places for three with their faces to the horses; and a bench across, from door to door, for three more. These were only nine places, even could they all be secured, which was doubtful: and nine places would not suffice to my party. Moreover, the coach started in the evening, and we should have to travel all that and the following night. It was not to be thought of.

"Do as we all do," said Mr. Turtle [proprietor of the Wright's House hotel, at which the Bestes were staying]. "Buy a wagon and a pair of horses, and drive across the prairie."

The spirit of adventure was upon us; and the idea was rather taking.

I had much difficulty in getting a wagon to my taste. I had, of course, understood that I was to have a spring wagon; but was now assured that no springs could stand the roughness of the

"My situation at Indianapolis, I found helpless. I had come by railway as far as railway could forward me in this direction."—J. Richard Beste

In due time, the railroad forwarded passengers all the way to the West Coast, eclipsing the National Road as the favorite route west. And in due course, the railroad itself was eclipsed by the automobile and the airline. Curiously Conestoga–shaped, the main waiting room of Indianapolis's Union Station today is a place to eat "Grand Brunch."

roads I should have to pass. To a wagon without springs, we had, therefore, to resign ourselves. I found an emigrant German wheelwright who had just finished a wagon, and paid for the whole as follows:

Indianapolis, June 26, 1851
TO: S. HETSELGESER

	Dolls.	Cents
For one wagon	65	0
" " bed	9	0
Making seat	1	0
Step and staples for seat	1	0
Making bows (for the cover)	2	0
For removes of shoes	0	50
	78	50

On the 27th of June, 1851, our beautiful horses started forth, with a will, on our journey across the prairies to the banks of the mighty Mississippi. Carpet-bags and such light articles were thrown into the bottom of our wagon, as we thought that they would make convenient seats for the children [heavier items being transported in a separate wagon]. The body of the vehicle was then filled half way up with hay and straw, that they might less feel the shaking and the jolting. The cages of the parrot and of the canary birds were tied to the hoops, on which the canvas awning was stretched, overhead: and, amid much fun and laughter, the children helped, lifted and tumbled one another into their places. My wife and I scrambled up to the bench, which I had made and swung across, on straps, under the awning in front. I handled my beautiful whip and shook the reins; and away our horses started at a good trot. The Indianapolitans looked after us admiring, and thought we had a most perfect turn out for the prairie and the backwoods.

We were, in truth, very happy.

But how felt our children?

"How delightful we all thought it for the first five minutes!" wrote Louie [in a separate diary]. "Eleven children packed in straw, with carpet-bags and dressing-cases filling up the crevices, and a canvas awning over our heads! In the exuberance of our spirits, we all sang, 'In the days when we went gypseying.' But, in a very short time, complaints and murmurs began to arise from all parties. 'How the wagon jolts!' cried one: 'How burning hot the sun is through the top!' exclaimed another: 'How uncomfortable it is not to have any seats!' said a third, moving impatiently."

"Like so many other poor friendless emigrants in America, here we had to undergo our trials and to fight the battle of life."—J. Richard Beste

An old engraving titled "The Emigrants."

"Before we had been three yards," wrote Lucy, "Polly's cage began swinging backwards and forwards amongst us, knocking the heads on each side of it; and the poor canaries were jolted off their perches to the bottom of their own cage. That we might not incommode the person opposite to each of us, we were obliged to draw our feet under us, like tailors, or to sit upon our heels; but then, if we leant against the sides of the wagon, we felt that the skin would soon be rubbed off our shoulders by its jolting. Fancy our position; with two little children tumbling in the hay and crawling over everybody, and that dreadful cage thumping our heads."

The road continued in a nearly straight direction through a pleasant country, in which cultivated spots amid the woods and prairies grew more and more rare. There was a good deal of traffic on the road, quite as much as would be seen on a turnpike road in England.

[In] Mount Meridian, a pretty little village [35 miles west of Indianapolis], we found a decent public house, the poor woman of which set out for us a tolerable breakfast, and attended on us as well as she could. But she too was suffering from the toothache; and was soon obliged to betake herself to the chimney corner, where she sat smoking a pipe of tobacco in the hope of relieving the pain.

After Mount Meridian, we found our road change sadly for the worse. It is true that it is marked in all the maps as the "National Road" leading from east to west in an almost straight line [but its condition] now depended upon the wants and the traffic of each township through which it passed. The tract of country after passing Mount Meridian was but thinly inhabited: the road was little used, and still less attention was given to keep it up. The water tables on each side were choked or washed away: water courses ran down the middle of it or furrowed it deep from side to side, or dug it into wide pits. Sometimes, these had to be passed through almost on stepping stones: sometimes the rain-channels were bridged over by planks, so short that there was not an inch to spare at the side of each wheel. Sometimes, where the gravelly top soil was quite worn away, and a quicksandy bottom exposed beneath, a track, just wide enough for the wheels, was made by a corduroy road laid across the bog. I have already explained the construction of a plank road: the difference between it and a corduroy road is much the same as that between a log and a frame house. A corduroy road is made of unhewn boles of trees laid side by side on the earth. A slip is nailed across each end to keep them in their places: and the wheels, whether of carriage or wagon, fall from bole to bole with the regularity of the thumps and stops with which the cogs in the wheels of a watch play into and arrest one another. Sometimes, the hollow between each prostrate trunk of a tree is partially filled up by earth; and then, of course, the jolts are less severe.

It was on Sunday morning, the 29th of June, that we arrived in Terre Haute. Having given directions that our horses should be baited, I went and sat me down in the hotel [Prairie House, on the National Road]; as I felt too unwell to accompany our children, who hoped still to reach church in time for Divine service.

At one o'clock, the hateful gong sounded through the "Prairie House," and we all went in to dinner. The eating-room was of handsome dimensions, well lighted by a row of windows on each side. The tables were laid out with great neatness and propriety.

After dinner, I did not feel any better; and we resolved, unwillingly, to spend the rest of this day here, and to move forwards on the following morning. Our children [having been too late for church that morning] started again to church for the afternoon service, and we selected our apartments in the hotel. I lay down on my bed while our children were at vespers.

I had an unquiet night; and, on the following morning felt that I could not continue our journey on that day. Meanwhile, [daughters] Louie and our little Isabel had not been quite well. The family medicine chest had been had recourse to; a small dose of the same medicine [blue pill and castor oil and laudanum] had been administered to each, and we nothing doubted but that all would be right the next day.

In the night, however, I was far from getting better. My wife wished to send for a doctor, and to this I strenuously objected, on the plea that I was certain that he would bleed me, and that this would surely kill me. She said that I had been delirious at the time: certainly this dread of being bled for a bowel complaint looked something like it: but I had been reading Dr. Dixon's book on *The Fallacies of the Faculty*. In the morning, however, it appeared that Isabel's state was far from satisfactory; and I immediately wrote a note to Dr. Read, requesting him to visit us.

In a few minutes, he stood by my bedside. A middle-sized, light-haired man of about forty years of age; with hollow cheeks and high American cheek bones; with long, lanky, brown hair that nearly hid his baldness; with a round, bright blue eye which he opened very wide and rolled about incessantly; with an inquisitive, intelligent, good-humoured and very animated look, Dr. Read thus stood by my bedside. With his two hands in his breeches pockets, his shocking bad hat upon his head, and a

The Prairie House, Terre Haute, as it would have appeared when the
Beste family stayed there. Built in 1837, it was demolished in the 1880s
for another hotel of the same name.

Courtesy of the Vigo County Historical Society

quid of tobacco in his mouth, which he twisted incessantly from side to side, while he occasionally squirted the juice to the floor on the other side of the room, Dr. Read thus stood by my bedside and examined me. My poor wife was horror-stricken. She thought we had got a wild man of the woods for a physician. However, the doctor, at length, felt my pulse and made all the usual inquiries; talked, apparently, very sensibly; assured us that my illness was nothing; and went with the mother to see our little girl.

Here the case was more serious. He pronounced her, at once, to be suffering from bloody dysentery; but still gave hopes that in a few days she would again be well.

Thus, instead of hurrying on after a stoppage of two hours, as we had first intended to do, here had we been already detained for two days; and here it was announced that we must remain for an indefinite period. Alone, in a village in the Far West, without a single acquaintance who had known us in former days—here we were stricken down like so many other poor friendless emigrants in America, here had we to undergo our trials and to fight the battle of life.

The illnesses continued; and a third and a fourth day we were detained at Terre Haute. It was necessary to divide the watches of the day and night. Catherine, our eldest daughter, constituted herself little Isabel's head nurse, assisted by our two next eldest girls; Louie and Agnes took charge of the two babies, four and two years old; Frank and his next youngest brother, aged ten, held themselves in readiness to run errands: my wife devoted herself to me. The three eldest sat up in turns throughout the night with their sister. Pain prevented the poor child from sleeping; and medicine had to be administered to her every half hour. All these she took without a murmur. Poor little thing! She had spent but nine years with us; as good and harmless a child as ever lived. Every one showed the greatest sympathy and kindness; not only the people of the hotel, but also the boarders in it; particularly a Mrs. Harrison, the wife of Colonel Harrison, grandson of a former President of the United States, who came constantly in the sick room of the child, and, with her mother, was of the greatest assistance.

The week passed on, and I seemed to grow better and worse; there was, in fact, no material change. Stupified by opium, excited by brandy and water, nourished by chicken broth, and chilled by lumps of ice; such were the strange remedies prescribed for me!

Meanwhile our eldest daughter seemed to be quite smitten down by the blow which had fallen upon the family, and by the real work and hardships which all had to undergo. She, who had always been a second mother to the younger ones, seemed unable to command her faculties to meet these new difficulties.

"In the watches of the night," [wrote daughter Lucy, in a separate account] "she could not remember what had passed before she went to sleep, or when to administer the different medicines; and was obliged, therefore, to give up her turn.

"On the eighth night, about one o'clock, I went to [Isabel's] bedside to look at our sufferer; and I cannot describe my feelings when I saw her. She was quite changed. All her features were pinched up, and death was written on her face. I had never before seen the dying.

"In the [next] afternoon, M. Lalumiere [the local priest] came and administered to her the sacrament of extreme unction. At first, she seemed insensible; but, by degrees, she appeared to waken up with a most beautiful smile, which became angelical as the priest pronounced the last blessing with the plenary indulgence.

"About half-past ten o'clock on Thursday morning, I found all my brothers and sisters on their knees. I knelt also; and, after a while, Catherine took a prayer-book and began reading prayers for a departing soul: but her voice faltered, and she was unable to continue. I took the book from her, and read on and watched dear Isabel while I read. Just as I finished the prayers, a heavenly smile passed over her face, and her pure soul left its prison and was borne to heaven.

"The church [for the funeral] was filled with people who knew us only by sight. Many [others] did not come into the church, but waited outside during the service, and then followed us to the burial-ground, which was nearly two miles distant. Thus many of this nation, who are said to think only of dollars and of going a-head, left their business during the best part of the day to follow, two miles to the grave, the little stranger of whom they knew nothing, and to show their sympathy for the family. Who will say that the Americans are not a kind-hearted people!

"It jarred dreadfully against our feelings to see the hearse jolted so fast over the uneven road: but this was not considered amiss by others. When we arrived at the burial-ground, we found the whole space filled with people who had walked or rode out there. All made way for us. The little grave was lined with planks; and a plank covering was let down over the coffin: these were their substitutes for a brick vault. In a short time, we left the body of our darling sister in an American graveyard."

[Early August—again in the words of the father, who, after four weeks in bed at the Prairie House, has largely recovered from dysentery or cholera:]

We resolved to return immediately to Europe; but the difficulty was, how to get there. I was told, and I felt, that I could not bear land carriage; and here we were eleven hundred miles from the sea of New York, and fifteen hundred from that of New Orleans. It was, also, considered necessary that I should rest and reside some little while in a cooler and more bracing climate before undertaking the whole of the journey to New York, or the sea voyage beyond.

There was a canal which united the Ohio River with Lake Erie. Running beside the Wabash to the shore of the Meaumee River, it passed through Terre Haute. Steamers, indeed, from the Ohio ascended the Wabash to Terre Haute and beyond, in the winter; but the waters were now getting too low for them. We were advised to go by the Wabash and Erie canal boats, which would carry us a distance of three hundred and twenty miles, and deliver us at Toledo on Lake Erie, in somewhat less than five days and five nights.

Having resolved to return by the Wabash and Erie canal boats, I sold my wagon, to the great joy of all my children. It was bought by one who wished to drive across the prairies to Chicago in it; and he gave me, within two dollars, what the whole had cost.

I paid my bill at the Prairie House. Five dollars a-week was charged for each grown-up person for board, lodging, and attendance. The charge for the servant was half that amount. Two dollars and a half, or ten shillings per week, was charged for each horse.

Getting into our carriage, we bade a long adieu to the red brick walls of the Prairie Hotel. At the canal wharf, we were soon rejoined by Dr. Read. Three horses were harnessed to the boat; we took a sad leave of our kind friend, and were soon passing through the water of the canal at the rate of from four to five miles per hour.

V. AND THEN
A WHISTLE

*The coming of the railroad signals
the decline of the National Road*

In an allegorical painting titled "The Meeting of the Ways," a stagecoach halts its travel to let an early railroad train pass.

A NEW NATIONAL ROAD

There is, wonderful to say, a railroad in process of construction over these mountains, and it is advancing with great rapidity.

It was 1847, and these were the very mountains that had both exhilarated and exhausted travelers of the National Road since its earliest days; and the observer, poignantly enough, was herself also a traveler of the National Road. Unlike her predecessors, Matilda Houstoun did not reach the National Road by horseback or coach or wagon or carriage. She "took the rail" to Cumberland, thence to travel the old-fashioned way—a way that would not long endure "the great rapidity" of change in travel.

And how could it? An 1840s stagecoach ride from Baltimore to Cumberland took more than twenty hours and cost $9. The Baltimore & Ohio Railroad now traveled the same route in less than ten hours for $7.

Even as the National Road was pushing into Ohio in the mid-1820s, the same movers and shakers—the bankers and businessmen of Baltimore—who, in 1797, had helped set the National Road in motion with creation of the privately financed Baltimore Pike were now setting in motion still a new era of travel. Meeting in Baltimore in February 1827, they faced the reality of quickly changing times. Highway transportation of goods and commodities was becoming more expensive compared with an emerging new form—the canal. Indeed, whereas Baltimore had been commercially competitive with other major cities since before the Revolution, it now risked being completely overshadowed by New York, which two years earlier had become a port for the Great Lakes by way of the just opened Erie Canal. A canal was not the answer for Baltimore because the only natural water route west serving Maryland was the Potomac River, and that would make Washington, not Baltimore, the beneficiary.

There was another possibility, still another new form of transportation that might move goods even faster and more cheaply than canal boats, indeed at speeds hitherto unknown to man. A brother of one of the Baltimore businessmen, living in England, wrote of the success of a railroad there between Stockton and Darlington that was successful enough hauling freight that another line was being built for passengers. Perhaps this was the answer, the Baltimore businessmen agreed; so, contemplating a new commercial link with the Ohio River, they established the Baltimore and Ohio Rail Road under charter from the state government. Within three years they had opened the first section to Ellicott's Mills, 10 miles west of Baltimore, using horse-drawn cars riding the rails; and four years later Harpers Ferry; and in 1844, Cumberland, now using steam-powered locomotives.

*   *   *

Matilda Houstoun, a young woman from England on a tour through America, and John Lewis Peyton, a Virginia-born author, were among those who took the railroad to Cumberland, and from there traveled the National Road the increasingly old-fashioned way—by horse-drawn coach.

MATILDA HOUSTOUN, 1847

By "Exclusive Extra" Coach, Cumberland to Brownsville

[Mid-November]
We hired a huge coach, [back in England] called an "extra," to convey us, on the morning following our arrival at Cumberland, across the Alleghany Mountains to Brownsville. The carriage was capable of carrying nine persons in its interior: a moveable board being arranged across the centre, with a broad leather band to support the back of those who, in public carriages, are unfortunate enough to form the middle part of this human sandwich. When a carriage of this description is engaged for a private party, it is dignified by the name of an "exclusive extra," the centre seat is removed, and you make yourself as comfortable as circumstances, and plenty of room, will admit of. The public stage is the usual mode of conveyance, for the Americans are too little susceptible of petty annoyances, and not

Brownsville today—a half-mile train of coal cars.

sufficiently alive to the delicacies of life, to find a carriage crowded with promiscuous company at all disagreeable, or to be willing to pay their dollars for empty places.

We set off on a lovely morning: there was a crisp and almost wintry feeling in the air, but the sun shone brightly, and the fresh breeze came wooingly down from the mountains, as if to bid us hasten up and enjoy it.

During the first three hours of our journey, we gradually ascended the whole way. We looked back occasionally from our leathern 'conveniency,' and gazed upon the glorious country which was lying far beneath us. There was also great and varied beauty in the forest scene around; here and there, we peered up dark and gloomy ravines, the farthest of which were lost in obscurity, and appeared to be intended by nature for what they probably were—namely, the favourite haunts of wolves and bears.

The carriage was very light, considering its size, and had wide leather springs, the only kind capable of supporting the violent shocks caused by the extreme badness of the road, with any degree of ease or comfort to the traveller. The unwieldy vehicle had a scarlet body, which was painted as fantastically as that of a red Indian, and on the panels were splendid and fanciful designs, of every colour of the rainbow. Our "team" consisted of four neat little, thorough-bred horses, who went at a great pace *up* the hills, but were allowed to take their own time in descending. The road, as I said before, was in a most wretched state—full of holes, deep ruts, and large stones, and, moreover, there is scarcely ever any level ground, hill succeeding hill in rapid succession. On either side there are frequently deep ravines, close to which the road passes, nor is there any fence between it and those frightful precipices. Fatal accidents are constantly occurring in these places, owing to the restiveness of horses, or to the carelessness, and almost proverbial recklessness of the stage drivers.

The comparative emptiness of our extensive vehicle had one manifest inconvenience—namely, that it greatly increased the difficulty of keeping ourselves in our places. It was impossible, for one moment, to lose sight of the absolute necessity for holding on, without being punished for our temporary negligence in a most signal manner. The great object was to prevent our heads coming in contact with the roof of the carriage, when any particularly violent jolt threw us with merciless force into the air. It was difficult to imagine any poor human beings more in the situation of shuttle-cocks. Side tumbles we could have borne better, but to be obliged to hold on with all our force to the seat, throughout the livelong day, for fear of having our heads knocked in, was rather too much of a travelling inconvenience. We suffered from nothing but great fatigue; but I have heard of sundry travellers who had been much less fortunate. I find no difficulty in believing all the stories of concussion of the brain and other frightful misadventures connected with stage travelling across the mountains.

We had not performed more than half our day's journey, when we began to perceive signs and symptoms that plainly denoted our entrance into a colder climate. Patches of unmelted snow lay among the dark and drooping leaves of the rhododendrons, and in sheltered places the shining ice glistened out among the grass. At some of the larger houses, we saw sledges, of various forms and kinds, brought out, as if in preparation for winter use, and skins of beasts hung out to dry in the still warm rays of a November sun.

Towards noon, we had one continued and very long ascent which lasted a couple of hours, and when we had surmounted it we found we had arrived at the center and highest ridge of the Alleghanys. We were now at the height of about two thousand seven hundred feet above the level of the sea, and thought it high time to bait our horses, and recruit our own strength by a little rest, and such a dinner as we could hope to obtain at so great an elevation above civilized life.

The inn at which our driver drew up, though calling itself, as a matter of course, a *hoetel,* did not, in its outward appearance, give much promise of good cheer within. On seeing us stop before his house, the landlord, a stout, burly mountaineer, came out to receive us with a cigar in his mouth, and the warmest welcome I ever met with, even in that proverbially hospitable place, an inn. On this occasion, however, we were fairly justified in suspecting his joy to be even somewhat more interested than such welcomes usually are, as the house was not one of the usual stopping places for the stages, and our advent was evidently quite an unlooked for blessing.

To our dismay, we found no fire in the chimney, which was as wide and high as those which we sometimes see in old farmhouses in England, and was adapted for burning wood alone. We had not, however, long to wait with chattering jaws and ruthless faces, for the landlord speedily appeared with his arms full of oak timber, and we were soon, one and all, speedily employed in blowing the welcome sparks into a blaze. The fire, which soon burned bright and cheerily, was most welcome to us after our mountain drive; for the sharp, north wind had blown keenly through the ill-fitting doors and windows of our huge glass-coach, and we were chilled to the bone. After a wonderfully short delay, the gentleman of the house appeared with the results of his culinary art, and, after all the apologies he had made for scantiness of provisions, &c., we were agreeably surprised, both at the quantity and quality of the food which was laid on the table. The main constituents of the feast were lumps of salted bear's meat *cold,* and some hot venison steaks of excellent quality.

After hoping that we would excuse the simplicity of our fare, which (with the addition of some delicious mountain honey) was all he had to offer, our host seemed to consider it a part of his duty to sit down with us, and do the honours of his table, ministering to our wants, and making himself agreeable according to the best of his ways and means. He was an intelligent man. Indeed, I have generally noticed that those who have energy sufficient to induce them to venture into still uncleared and unsettled districts, are almost always endowed with considerable powers of mind and great faculties of observation. He was a regular Yankee, except in his dimensions, which were more worthy of the lengthy race of "old Kentuck." Though in this solitary and necessarily hardworking situation, he still wore the invariable black silk waistcoat and broad-toed dancing-boots, which I have noticed alike as worn by the settler on the muddy banks of the Mississippi, and by the New England farmer, even when working themselves in their diggings and clearings. But to return to our rather amusing dinner. Our drink was water from the spring, with rye whisky, in case we should happen to have no taste for so simple a beverage; and our talk was of Oregon, California, the chances of war, sporting, and taxation. Altogether, the conversation was far from uninstructive, neither was it dull; and I could not help thinking how differently a man, belonging to the same class in England, would in all probability have behaved if placed in similar circumstances.

There is, wonderful to say, a railroad in process of construction over these mountains, and it is advancing with great rapidity, considering the vast impediments which lie in the way of its completion. As in our own country, as well as further north in *this,* the labourers employed are mostly Irish; and a very sad set they are. Paddy cannot be quiet, let him be where he will; and nowhere is he more thoroughly outrageous than in this "land of liberty." Their wages are, unfortunately, high, and rye whiskey, still more unfortunately cheap, so that they have little chance of behaving well, or quietly.

We journeyed on through the second day with no variety in the scenery, and nothing to remark upon, except that the road became worse every moment, and that our heads and limbs were in greater and more imminent danger than ever.

We had gone on in so very monotonous a manner for several

The Mount Washington Tavern, near Farmington, Pennsylvania: a gaming table.

hours, that we were beginning to lose all interest in what was in itself so uninteresting as this stage of our journey, when the carriage suddenly stopped. The sun had just reached his meridian, and after a dull and threatening morning, was peeping out for the first time between his curtains of clouds, when our attention was attracted by this unexpected halt. We looked out, and what a change of prospect was before us! We had emerged from the dark forests, and, to our great surprise, were looking down upon the vast plains beneath us. Far and wide, and on every side, stretched the vast expanse of country: and cultivated lands, and broad shining rivers, and thriving towns, with spires glistening in the sunshine, all were spread, as in a vast panorama, before us. The driver looked into the carriage, and pointed all these things out to us, and verily, he seemed as proud of the beautiful prospect before him, as is the Italian postilion when he introduces a traveller to his first glimpse of the eternal city.

We were a long time creeping down the long hill to Union Town. The road is beautifully made, throughout the entire descent, but it is nevertheless very steep, and our driver, partly perhaps because the horses were his own, and partly from the admixture of Scotch caution, (for he was from the *canny* side of the Tweed,) tempering the fire of Yankee recklessness, drove very slowly and carefully. The view varied with every turn in the road, and after a while, cottages (picturesque ones, too) by the wayside, became gradually more frequent, and symptoms of civilization increased rapidly. About two o'clock in the afternoon, we entered Union Town, a clean, nice-looking village, for it is as yet nothing more, with quite an English inn at the entrance. We asked for dinner, and they brought us the infallible beefsteak, and the cornbread, the *no* wine, and the offer of new milk. Fresh eggs, however, were plentiful—so we had not, after all, much reason to complain.

After resting the horses for a couple of hours, we proceeded through a flat and very unpicturesque country to Brownsville, where we were to pass the night. I have forgotten to mention to you that, during this our last day's journey, we passed by "Great Meadows," a spot rendered interesting from the fact of its having been the field where Washington was first engaged in battle. A heap of stones was pointed out to us as Braddock's grave, and this was the only sign or vestige that remained of Fort Necessity, a defence which was erected by Washington, and afterwards abandoned to the Indians. Ninety-three years ago, Washington had marched by nearly the same route over which we had travelled since we left Cumberland. In those early days they had frequently to hack and hew their way through the thick and entirely uncleared forest, and those who have the misfortune to pass over the same mountain road *now*, (when so much has been done to render the way comparatively easy), can form some slight idea of the difficulties which in those days lay in the path of the advancing army.

Brownsville is a most dirty town, dirty with smoke, and coal, and manufactures. It stands on the Monongahela river, across which is thrown a rather handsome bridge. We found our hotel remarkably comfortable. There was no appearance of public dining, ordinaries, or "ladies' parlour;" and we had a sitting room to ourselves, opening into a pretty and well-kept garden, and a sleeping apartment within it, which was fitted up with every comfort. Our evening meal (*tea* is an important repast with the Americans) consisted of delicious kinds of bread, both corn and wheat, preserves of many sorts, strawberry, apricot, and peach, rich cream, and excellent tea. The latter luxury is almost always good in this country. I must not, in this enumeration of the "delicacies of the season," forget to mention with respect a sort of pancake, which we had at Brownsville, in the greatest perfection: it is made of Indian corn, and is brought in very hot, and in relays. It is, I fancy, called a "Johnny cake," and is generally eaten with molasses; but it is excellent with fresh butter, and is, I believe, one of the causes of the brevity of human existence here. Our attendant was a neat-handed little damsel of ten years old; she was a pretty intelligent child, and the niece of the landlord. In any other country she would have been still in the nursery, but here, where everything and everybody are precocious, she was head waiter, chambermaid, and, for aught I know to the contrary, housekeeper besides.

Every one we met in the town of Brownsville had a face more or less begrimed with smoke and coal-dust. Altogether, it reminded me very much of some parts of my own dear country. And the next morning, as we stood upon the wharf, waiting for the steamer that was to convey us down the [Monongahela] river [to Pittsburgh], I could have fancied myself in a Staffordshire village, with the dingy-faced coal-workers around me.

JOHN LEWIS PEYTON, 1848
By Stagecoach, Cumberland to Brownsville

[From an 1848 diary; written as a memoir and published in 1869]

[Late June]
Our delay at Harper's Ferry was not protracted longer than was necessary to visit the public works and the most striking

John Lewis Peyton

scenery in the immediate vicinity. Having accomplished these objects we resumed our journey west, by the Baltimore and Ohio railway. A few hours brought us to Cumberland, which was the terminus of the road and the furthest point west that any railway in the Southern States had then attained. Here we turned out of the cars to enter the stage-coach. Beyond this point there was a highway called "The National Road," because constructed by the United States' Government, connecting the town with the west. Seating ourselves in the vehicle we jogged on through rugged, mountainous country, a distance of about a hundred miles, to the valley of the Monongahela river.

Some of the scenery on this route is grand, all of it diversified, romantic and beautiful. The mountains were heavily timbered with oak, pine and cedar. The underwood was generally very thick, the ground between the trees being covered with mountain laurel, so luxuriant, too, was the growth of this and other plants, that the woods were in many places impenetrable. Panthers, bears, wolves, deer, elk, and many other kinds of wild animals were found in these uplands as still they are. Notwithstanding an occasional clearing and a rude hut, with a cow and a few pigs grazing around it, the country was perfectly "wild." Among the most venomous reptiles in these regions are the rattlesnakes, and they exist in such numbers that it is next to impossible to shoot in the mountains during the summer, and land is never surveyed at this season owing to the terror they inspire. A short distance beyond Smithfield, near the road side, we passed the spot where General Braddock was interred after his defeat and death; our road, indeed, pursued the exact line of march of this unfortunate leader. The ascent commenced almost immediately after leaving Cumberland. Our present road and the means of locomotion, primitive as they unquestionably must at this day be regarded, were greatly in advance of his time. One of the officers [Captain Orme] who accompanied Braddock's expedition, writing from Monakatuka Camp, July 1755, says, "we encounter every kind of difficulty. Frequently we have had to cut our road through the pathless forest, and to let our baggage and waggons down steep precipices by ropes and pulleys."

At this day a railway has been constructed across these Virginian Alps, rivalling in its grades and the physical difficulties surmounted, that of Mount Cenis. Where the savage trod in 1755, and the stage-coach dragged its slow length along in 1848, the train sweeps by in 1869, bearing thousands of passengers daily on their journeys, and transporting hundreds of thousands of tons of freight. We live in a fast age it must be allowed. Old things have passed away—all things become new.

A GLORY DEPARTED

The great National Road was altogether giving way now to the *new* national road—the one that was sweeping up the nation in a frenzy of travel at hitherto unknown quotients of time and distance. "Westward ho!" exulted a writer in the June 1859 issue of *Harper's*. His story was about an excursion train that had stopped briefly in Cumberland to allow time for "wandering in the hills" and for "episodical excursions to Frostburg and Mount Savage," from which all "returned well pleased with what they had seen"—the sort of thing stagecoach passengers used to do.

"Westward, ho!, with exhilarating speed," he rejoiced, "diving deeper and deeper into the mountains." During the 1850s alone, the nation's burgeoning railroad system not only was diving into the mountains but shooting up and down the Atlantic Seaboard and across the coastal plain and over the foothills, adding more than 21,000 miles to the nation's rail network. That was nearly ten times as much trackage as existed in 1840. By 1854, the railroad had met the Mississippi; and in 1869, East met West by rail at Promontory, Utah. Construction reached new peaks, with more than 70,000 route-miles of rail added during the 1880s alone.

* * *

Meanwhile, the National Road, hardly national in significance anymore, was becoming even less of a road. Mile after mile could be passed now without a sight of one of its famous old inns; and where there was a reminder, it was usually a dilapidated old place with windows nodding through half-closed shutters. The road surface was often a mosaic of moss and weeds; and the once brisk staccato of horseshoes on stone pavement had given way to the gentle pipings of songbirds in overhanging branches— gentle sounds too soft to be heard in the fortissimo of the road's great years.

By the 1870s, even the various states no longer wanted the old road; so, one by one, they began turning responsibility over to the counties. For the most part, the counties, figuring that toll collecting was more trouble than it was worth now with so little use, stopped collecting tolls (although on some sections, tolls remained until as late as 1910). The counties either tried to get local government to take responsibility or simply let maintenance taper off to outright neglect.

What was it like to travel now—this great old road linking east to west? What indeed! wondered this same *Harper's* in

"Lapsed into the oblivion of its years."

Harper's Magazine, November 1879

"A mosaic of moss and weeds." The National Road bridge east of New Concord, Ohio as it is today.

1879, as correspondent William H. Rideing set out by hired coach to see the old national road as the new one entered its heyday.

WILLIAM HENRY RIDEING, 1879

By Hired Carriage, Frederick to Cumberland

The national turnpike that led over the Alleghanies from the East to the West is a glory departed, and the traffic that once belonged to it now courses through other channels; but it is not simply because it is past that a few old men living who have resminiscences of it glow with excitement and exalt it in recalling them. Aroused out of the dreamy silence of their ebbing days by a suggestion of it, the octogenarians who participated in the traffic will tell an inquirer that never before were there such landlords [innkeepers], such taverns, such dinners, such whiskey, such bustle, or such endless cavalcades of coaches and wagons as could be seen or had between Wheeling and Frederick in the palmy days of the old national "pike;" and it is certain that when coaching days were palmy, no other post-road in the country did the same business as this fine old highway, which opened the West and Southwest to the East. The wagons were so numerous that the leaders of one team had their noses in the trough at the end of the next wagon ahead; and the coaches, drawn by four or six horses, dashed along at a speed of which a modern limited express might not feel ashamed. Besides the coaches and wagons, there were gentlemen travelling singly in the saddle, with all the accoutrements of the journey stuffed into their saddle-bags; and there were enormous droves of sheep and herds of cattle, which raised the dust like a cloud along their path.

We have written of what is past. The canal and the railway have superseded the old national "pike," and it is not often now that a traveller disturbs the dust that lies upon it. The dust itself, indeed, has settled and given root to the grass and shrubbery, which in many places show how complete the decadence is. The black snakes, moccasins, and copperheads, that were always plentiful in the mountains, have become so unused to the intrusion of man that they sun themselves in the road, and a vehicle can not pass without running over them. Many of the villages which were prosperous in the coaching days have fallen asleep, and the wagon of a peddler or farmer is alone seen where once the travel was enormous. The men who were actively engaged on the road as drivers, station agents, and mail contractors are nearly all dead. The few that remain are very old, and while an inquiry about the past re-animates them for a moment, they soon lapse into the oblivion of their years. But the taverns, with their hospitable and picturesque fronts, the old smithies, and the tollgates, have not been entirely swept away. Enough has been left undespoiled to sustain the interest and individuality of the highway.

In a journey last summer we made Frederick our starting-point, and entered it from the fertile meadows basined in the Blue Ridge, which are as sunny and as tranquil as the description of them in Whittier's poem.

We hired a team to Cumberland. The driver assigned to us was named Leander, and with this pretty name he had a bullet-like head, close-cropped, and a villainous countenance which belied a most amiable disposition.

Leander's whip cracked, and Frederick was soon invisible in the foliage which engirths it. Placid meadows were on both sides of us; the Blue Ridge was like a cloud in the south, and ahead of us was the famous highway, dipping and rising by many alternations toward a hazy line of hills in the west, like a thread of white drawn through the verdant meadows. The chestnuts made arches over it, and divided its borders with tulip poplars and blossoming locusts, which filled the air with fragrance. A Roman highway buried under the farmlands of England could not be much more in contrast with the activity of its past than this. The winding undulations revealed no travellers; some of the old taverns with windows gaped vacantly, while a few others were occupied; a part of the toll-houses were abandoned, and those which do double duty find so little business that the keeper combines his occupation with that of the cobbler or blacksmith.

Hagerstown has suffered little by the withdrawal of the coaches; it is the busy and crowded seat of a Maryland county; but its old citizens lament the change, and cherish their reminiscences of the days when the "pike" was in its glory.

"From here to Boonsborough," said Mr. Eli Mobley, an old coach-maker, to us, "the road was the finest in the United States, and I have seen the mail-coaches travel from Hagerstown to Frederick, twenty-six miles, in two hours. That was not an unusual thing either; and there were through freight wagons from Baltimore to Wheeling which carried ten ton, and made nearly as good time as the coaches. They were drawn by twelve horses, and the rear wheels were ten feet high.

"I've seen Clay and Jackson often; neither of them was handsome, and one thing that strikes me is the fidelity of all the likenesses I've seen of 'em. Jackson and his family came along

Uncle Sam Ninny

Harper's Magazine, November 1879

quite often, the family in a private carriage, and the general on horseback, which he changed now and then for a seat in the vehicle. He was very fond of horses, and his own were something to look at."

Another survivor of the old "pike" is Samuel Ninny—a patriarchal African, who "played tambourine" for General Jackson, and drove on the road for many years. He is an odd mixture of shrewdness, intelligence, and egotism. His recollections are vivid and detailed in point of names and dates, although he is eighty-six years old, and he describes his experiences in a grandiose manner that is occasionally made delicious by solecisms, or sudden lapses into negro colloquialisms. He lives in a comfortable cottage at Hagerstown; the walls of his parlor are hung with certificates of membership in various societies, and with various patriotic chromos; the centre table is loaded with books, principally on negro emancipation and the events of the civil war.

West of Cumberland the road was bordered by an extraordinary growth of pines, the branches of which were so intermeshed that they admitted very little daylight, and from its prevailing darkness the grove was called the "Shades of Death." Uncle Sam Ninny and others declare that on the most effulgent day not a ray ever penetrated it, and that it was *absolutely black,* which is a piece of picturesque exaggeration. It was very dark, however, according to the statements of more exact observers, including Mr. B.F. Reinhart, the well-known painter, and it afforded a favorable opportunity for highwaymen. "I had a very keen team, Sir," says Uncle Sam—"a very keen team indeed; and nobody knows more about a horse than I do. I drove that team, Sir, nine months without the least sickness to the horses, and I flatter myself that we had some rough service." The flattery that Uncle Sam applies to himself is immense. "Well, Sir, one night I was driving through the Shades of Death with a few passengers; it was darker than usual; it was Cimmerian—*Cimmerian,* Sir; and one said to me, 'Don't you hear the sound of horses walking?' I listened, and listened, and listened. I *did* hear the sound of walking, and seemed to see, although it was so dark, several figures in the wood. Some one then opened the pistol case [in the coach] and examined the weapons; the flint had been removed from each pistol, and *about that time, Sir, my hair began to get curly.* The passengers didn't like the way affairs were looking; and I thought that if big men were scared, there was no reason why a little one shouldn't be scared too." Uncle Sam is very diminutive; and after acknowledging his trepidation, he repeated, in a manner of great candor: "I admit it, Sir, I *was* scared; and I just assure you, gentleman, that I made every

Highway robbers were an ever-present hazard of travel on the National Road in its heyday. A particularly notorious location was the "Shades of Death" east of Meadow Mountain in Maryland.

Harper's Magazine, November 1879 ("Preparing for Highwaymen")

horse tell [run its fastest] until we came to a tavern. But I wasn't naturally timid: I was puzzled as to how the flints came out of those pistols, and we could never unravel the mystery."

Beyond Hagerstown, the road is level and uninteresting, save for the capacious taverns, mostly in disuse, [and] the stables and smithies, which time has left standing.

If the road between Hagerstown and Clear Spring is unattractive, between Clear Spring and Hancock it approaches in beauty the grandest passes of the Sierras; and to paraphrase a witty antithesis of Aldrich's, if there is a more charming journey in the world than from Clear Spring to Hancock, it must be from Hancock to Clear Spring. There is a salient resemblance between the scenery of the Alleghanies and that of the Sierras. The two ranges have the same dusky and balsamic profusion of evergreens, the same deep and ever-silent glens imprisoned by almost sheer walls of pine, the same continuity and multiplicity of ridges, and in many other superficial points the similarity is sustained.

At the summit of Sidling Hill there is an immense prospect of ridges beyond ridges, visible along their whole length, which look like the vast waves of a petrified ocean. The basin disclosed is of extraordinary extent, and the mountains are crowded together, with little more than gorges between, in which lie depths of blue and purple haze. The turmoil of traffic here, the beat of hoofs, the rumble of wheels, the tintinnabulations of the teamsters' bells, the bellowing of cattle, the bleating of sheep, and the cries of the drovers, once so familiar, would now sound strangely inappropriate; but even in the travellers of long ago a thrill of novelty must have been excited by the stream of commerce flowing through these mountain confines.

Hancock, which was one of the busiest villages on the road, is now lugubriously apathetic, and the citizens sit before their doors with their interest buried in the past. The main street is silent, and the stables are vacant. No one who ever travelled over the road can fail to remember the many excellences of Ben Bean's, which stood midway on the main street. The old house is still standing, in much the same condition that it always was—with a long white front shaded with chestnuts and locusts, with a trough of water rippling before the door, with a breezy and commodious porch, and with low-ceilinged apartments, cleanly sanded. But Ben Bean has long been gathered to his fathers, and the gayety and activity that made his tavern in a measure famous have left no echo. His successors are two precise and elderly nieces, who entertain summer boarders, and are timid about transient customers. The little alcove in the tap-room, where the glasses, flasks, and demijohns confronted the thirsty and exhausted traveller, is closed beyond appeal;

perhaps that is for the better; but the tinkling of glasses and the hearty interchange of greetings and compliments that enlived the room of old seem more desirable than the present vacancy and silence. Between Hancock and Cumberland the road is almost deserted, and there is no tavern in over forty miles.

The sun had gone down when we attained the next summit; but we were received for the night in an old farm-house by a grizzled old farmer. "Can you give us something good for supper?" we eagerly inquired. "Well," said he, with readiness, "that depends upon what you consider good. Some folks are satisfied with pig and bread; others turn up their noses at beefsteak and onions. I've seen a man sneer at boiled pork and turnips. Now we ain't got anything as good as that: but we've good milk and bread and ham." We would have been glad to compromise with him on something much inferior to the supper he served us; and when we had eaten we sat with him on his porch, where we could hear the throbbing note of the whip-poor-will and the ghostly screech of the owls. It was intensely quite and lonely on the mountain. A herd of tame deer browsed about the garden, and once or twice we heard a sound like that of a wild-cat in the dense woods surrounding. The old farmer talked about the "pike." "The loss of it isn't very bad," he said. "When it was at its height all the people along here depended on it for a living, and now they're driven to farmin', which is much better for them." We slept well, partitioned from a numerous family by a board; there were a few insects, but we had become accustomed to much larger numbers, and after breakfast in the morning we paid our bill, which was not exorbitantly fixed at seventy-five cents, and resumed our journey, reaching Cumberland early in the afternoon.

Cumberland benefited largely by the "pike," especially when it was the western terminus of the Baltimore and Ohio Railway, and the point of transfer for passengers and freight going further west or east. A paragraph in the local annals announces that "the extent of passenger travel over the national road during 1849 was immense, and the reports of the agents show that from the 1st to the 20th of March the number of persons carried was 2586." Four years later, in 1853, the same annals announce the completion of the railway to Wheeling. "The effect was soon felt in Cumberland, as most of the stage lines were taken off, and the great business of transfering merchandise at this point was largely diminished. But while Cumberland was the busiest depot on the "pike" when that route was superseded, it continued to succeed through other resources, and it is now an active town.

West of Cumberland the national road proper extends to

Wheeling, partly following the route of General Braddock, who has left an interesting old mile-stone at Frostburg. The old iron gates have been despoiled, but the uniform toll-houses, the splendid bridges, and the iron distance posts show how ample the equipment was. The coaches ceased running in 1853: the "June Bug," the "Good Intent," and the "Landlord's," as the various lines were called, sold their stock, and a brilliant era of travel was ended.

Indiana

Indianapolis
Richmo

VI. A ROAD
NOW A MEMORY

*A byway forgotten, except to those
who liked to reminisce*

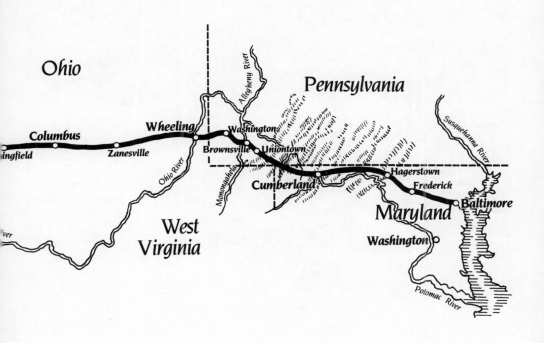

Looking west toward Chestnut Ridge, Pennsylvania, 1900.

A TIME TO REMEMBER

Gone the June Bug and the Good Intent and all the other stages, fast-flying, gaily painted ... Gone the heavy-laden Conestoga wagon, canvas flapping ... Gone the twelve-horse freighter, axles creaking ...

Gone the swift horse, the plodding mule ... the carriage and the Dearborn wagon ... the circus caravan and roving gypsies ... droves of fatted hogs, dust clouds rising ... the mail coach and the pack train ...

Gone the presidents in triumphal procession—Zachary Taylor, the last to travel the National Road inaugural-bound, did so in 1849, soon after the railroad reached Cumberland.

Yet not all was gone. Those cavities and declivities and awful furrows—they were still there, and worse than ever. The National Road (still so called) of the turn of the century was in many places impassable. Maintenance now was entirely local, and while some jurisdictions tried to keep the road in passable condition, most gave it only the scantest attention. The overall result was a road with no pretense of cross-country travel, or even cross-county travel in many cases.

* * *

There was little to do but reminisce about the glorious years, even if accepting them as "dead and gone," as did poet James Whitcomb Riley; or trace the old thread once again, as did author and scholar Rufus Rockwell Wilson, only to be "a silent watcher over the dead artery."

Greenup, Indiana, 1911

National Archives

West of Zanesville, Ohio, 1913

National Archives

James Whitcomb Riley

Library of Congress

JAMES WHITCOMB RILEY, 1897
Recollections; Greenfield, Indiana

A Child-World, yet a wondrous world no less,
To those who knew its boundless happiness.
A simple old frame house—eight rooms in all—
Set just one side the center of a small
But very hopeful Indiana town,—
The upper-story looking squarely down
Upon the main street, the main highway
From East to West,—historic in its day,
Known as The National Road—old-timers, all
Who linger yet, will happily recall
It as the scheme and handiwork, as well
As property, of "Uncle Sam," and tell
Of its importance, "long and long afore
Railroads wuz ever *dreamp'* of!"—Furthermore,
The reminiscent first inhabitants
Will make that old road blossom with romance
Of snowy caravans, in long parade
Of covered vehicles, of every grade
From ox-cart of most primitive design,
To Conestoga wagons, with their fine
Deep-chested six-horse teams, in heavy gear,
High hames and chiming bells—to childish ear
And eye entrancing as the glittering train
Of some sun-smitten pageant of Old Spain.
And, in like spirit, haply they will tell
You of the roadside forests, and the yell
Of "wolfs" and "painters," in the long night-ride,
And "screechin' catamounts" on every side.—
Of stagecoach-days, highwaymen, and strange crimes,
And yet unriddled mysteries of the times
Called "Good Old." "And why 'Good Old'?" once a rare
Old chronicler was asked, who brushed the hair
Out of his twinkling eyes and said,—"Well John,
They're 'good old times' because they're dead and gone!"

The home of James Whitcomb Riley in Greenfield, Indiana—an old view, with Conestoga wagon (one of the "snowy caravans in long parade") passing by.

In the 1920s, the home of James Whitcomb Riley as it appears in a photograph hanging in the home.

RUFUS ROCKWELL WILSON, 1902
By Horse and Carriage, Frederick to Brownsville

The coming of the railroad a generation and a half ago consigned the National Pike to the limbo of abandoned things. During a recent trip over it, few travellers were to be met with. Old taverns fast falling to ruins gape on either side; and the toll-keeper has little to do, while most of the pikeboys are dead or bending under the weight of years.

Our trip began at the fine old town of Frederick, in itself one of the romances of the National Pike, for there once dwelt Francis Scott Key, author of the "Star Spangled Banner," and aged Barbara Frietchie, the lion-hearted dame made immortal by Whittier's verse.

The journey westward over the National Pike, especially if it be taken in the green and fragrant month of June, is sure to dwell long and pleasantly in the memory. From Frederick placid meadows stretch away on either side to the horizon line, while to the south the distant, azure-tinted Blue Ridge looks like a low-lying truncated cloud.

From Hagerstown to Clear Spring, the pike is level and uninteresting, save for the roomy, dolorous taverns and the stables and smithies which time has left standing; but between Clear Spring and Hancock it rivals in beauty and grandeur the noblest passes of the Sierras, ridge flanking ridge until earth and sky meet and blend in cloud and mist.

Hancock, formerly a busy and bustling burg, is now as silent and somnolent as the thoroughfare which gave it birth, while from that point to Cumberland the pike is almost deserted, there being no tavern in over forty miles of a wild region, that during the war was a favorite ground of the bushwhackers. West of Cumberland, the pike pushes through a hill country, closely following as far as Uniontown, Pennsylvania, the route of General Braddock—who has left an interesting old milestone at Frostburg—passing the ruins of Fort Necessity and skirting the spot where the British commander was buried.

Our ride ended at the little town of Brownsville, just without the shadow of the Alleghanies' western slope. The story of this almost forgotten hamlet is another romance of the National Pike. Time was when the name of Brownsville was as familiar to the people of the West as that of Pittsburg, for which it was then the point from which a voyage down the Ohio and Mississippi was begun. Brownsville claimed the first steamer that ever ascended these rivers, and for the better part of two decades was the strong rival to Pittsburg, sixty-five miles to the north of it. Travellers coming from the South and West by water took passage over the pike at Brownsville, and wayfarers from the East began their river voyaging at that point. The older residents of the village retain many interesting recollections of that vanished time. For instance, when a steamboat from the West came within two miles of the town, the pilot blew his whistle, as many times as he had passengers for the East, thus notifying innkeepers and pike-boys how many people they would have to provide for. The signal also served to notify the townsfolk that a boat was about to arrive, and by the time it reached its wharf a great crowd was usually gathered to greet the incoming passengers.

Brownsville rose and fell with the National Pike, and the decline of the latter left it stranded on the shore that is washed by the sea of Buried Hopes. Nothing happens now in Brownsville, and never will. Grass is growing in its streets, and time and the elements are hastening its decay. I can think of it only as a silent watcher over the dead artery of trade from which it had its being.

"SOMETHING SWOOPING DOWN THE ROAD..."

Grass in the street or no, the significance of the old road was never entirely lost on successive generations. The old road was an engineering triumph of its day; it was as close to "straight as an arrow" as any road yet built; it was a splendidly chosen route; it was *uniquely a national highway.*

And moreover, there were still those tangible reminders of it: the old mileposts, here and there; antique but functional macadam, even if laced with moss and grass; and surely those "monumental relics of the old stone bridge builders' art," those Romanesque ruins that still carried an occasional farm wagon wandering about the old road.

And there were those who, seeing the tangible reminders, suspected the old road hadn't contributed the last of its usefulness— historian Archer Hulbert, for example, examining at first hand this "ancient elevated pathway of the gods"; or writer William Bayard Hale, returning to his childhood home on the National Road in Richmond, Indiana, and finding a new era "swooping down."

"Brownsville: just without the shadow of the Alleghanies' western slope, an almost forgotten hamlet."—Rufus Rockwell Wilson

The National Road just east of Brownsville, 1910.

Library of Congress

Archer Butler Hulbert

Courtesy, Special Collections,
The Colorado College

ARCHER BUTLER HULBERT, 1903

Partly on Foot, Partly by Carriage, Cumberland through Indiana

[As for the old road as seen by travelers today:] One cannot go a single mile without becoming deeply impressed with the evidence of the age and the individuality of the old Cumberland Road. There is nothing like it in the United States. Leaping the Ohio at Wheeling, the Cumberland Road throws itself across Ohio and Indiana, straight as an arrow, like an ancient elevated pathway of the gods, chopping hills in twain at a blow, traversing the lowlands on high grades like a railroad bed, vaulting river and stream on massive bridges of unparalleled size. The farther one travels upon it, the more impressed one must become.

For long distances, this road will be, so far as the immediate surface is concerned, what the tender mercies of the counties through which it passes will allow, but at certain points, the traveler comes out unexpectedly upon the ancient roadbed, for in many places the old macadamized bed is still doing noble duty.

Nothing is more striking than the ponderous stone bridges which carry the roadway over the waterways. It is doubtful if there are on this continent such monumental relics of the old stone bridge builders' art. Not only such massive bridges as those at Big Crossings and the artistic "S" bridge near Claysville, Pennsylvania, will attract the traveler's attention, but many of the less pretentious bridges over brooks and rivulets will, upon examination, be found to be ponderous pieces of workmanship.

The traveler will notice still the mileposts which mark the great road's successive steps. Those on the eastern portion of the road are of iron and were made at the foundries at Connellsville and Brownsville. Those between Brownsville and Cumberland have recently been reset and repainted. The milestones west of the Ohio River are mostly of sandstone, and are fast disappearing under the action of the weather. Some are quite illegible though the word "Cumberland" at the top can yet be read on almost all. In Central Ohio, through the Darby woods, or "Darby Cuttings," the mileposts have been greatly mutilated by vandal woodchoppers, who knocked off large chips with which to sharpen their axes.

The bed of the Cumberland Road was originally eighty feet in width [west of the Ohio River, but 66 feet to the east]. In Ohio at least, property owners have encroached upon the road until, in some places, ten feet of ground has been included within the fences. This matter has been brought into notice where franchises for electric railway lines have been granted. In Franklin

County, west of Columbus, Ohio, there is hardly room for a standard gauge track outside the roadbed, where once the road occupied forty feet each side of its axis. When the property owners were addressed with respect to the removal of their fences, they demanded to be shown quitclaim deeds for the land, which, it is unnecessary to say, were not forthcoming from the state. Hundreds of contracts, calling for a width of eighty feet, can be given as evidence of the original width of the road. In days when it was considered the most extraordinary good fortune to have the Cumberland Road pass through one's farm, it was not considered necessary to obtain quitclaim deeds for the land.

What of the future? The dawning of the era of country living is in sight. It is being hastened by the revolution in methods of locomotion. The bicycle and automobile presage an era of good roads, and of an unparalleled countryward movement of society. With this era is coming the revival of inn and tavern life, the rejuvenation of a thousand ancient highways and all the happy life that was ever known along their dusty stretches. By its position with reference to the national capital, and the military and commercial key of the Central West, Pittsburg, and both of the great cities of Ohio, the Cumberland Road will become, perhaps, the foremost of the great roadways of America. The bed is capable of being made substantial at a comparatively small cost, as the grading is quite perfect. Its course measures the shortest possible route practicable for a roadway from tidewater to the Mississippi River. As a trunk line its location cannot be surpassed. Its historic associations will render the route of increasing interest to the thousands who, in other days, will travel, in the genuine sense of the word, over those portions of its length which long ago became hallowed ground. The "Shades of Death" will again be filled with the echoing horn which heralded the arrival of the old-time coaches, and Winding Ridge again be crowded with the traffic of a nation. A hundred Cumberland Road taverns will be opened, and bustling landlords welcome, as of yore, the travel-stained visitor. Merry parties will again fill those tavern halls, now long silent, with their laughter.

WILLIAM BAYARD HALE, 1911
Richmond, Indiana

They talk much nowadays of good roads; they hold national congresses about them and publish magazines and memorialize legislatures about them; I believe the good roads idea has even become a movement.

Bless me! it did not remain for this generation to build good roads even in America. Has everybody forgotten that splendid highway which, before the day of the locomotive, the Government at Washington threw across the Alleghanies and pushed to the Mississippi—forgotten the romance and history that flowed over it, forgotten the surge of that fulfilling tide of civilization which, after the Revolution, found its outlet to the imperial West past the mile-stones that stretched—and stretch today— from Cumberland on the Potomac to St. Louis on the Father of Waters? Some of us have not forgotten.

It ran past the gate on which as a boy I used to swing on long summer days. Its direction gave the road an indubitable connection with the eternal structure of the universe, for the very sun seemed to travel it, coming along every morning out of the east, just as did the trains of canvas-canopied wagons, bound for Kansas, Colorado, or California. They were the most wonderful caravans in the world; it were not fit to mention with the trains of richly laden camels that brought to Mediterranean seaports the spoil of African mines and Persian looms. For these were freighted with expectation of fortunes vaster than anything the Old World had seen, though all you could discern with the physical eye was a line of long, low-hanging, pot-bellied vans arched over with bulging canvas gathered at each end, and with a stovepipe sticking hospitably out behind. They were drawn by teams of stout horses, with, like as not, a colt playing about the slow progress, and always a disconsolate dog under the wagon, a brace of boys and possibly a slatternly woman accompanying on foot, and with occasionally a canvas inscribed, if the "mover" was sentimental or humorous, with some such motto as "Westward Ho!" or "Pike's Peak or bust!"

Under the boughs of catalpa-trees and silver-leaf poplars to the eastward one could see up the old road a good mile to the top of the rise over which it disappeared into the great unknown, followed by an imagination which nothing else in all after life ever so powerfully awakened or so constantly allured. What wonders lay beyond the crest of Linden Hill, in that mysterious country whence the sun, whence "the movers," came?

*   *   *

During one period of each year, in particular, the capacity of the National Road seemed tried to its limit by processions of family carriages of the type possessed by every well-to-do Western family. They were filled with quakers coming to Yearly Meeting.

William Bayard Hale

The Whitewater Yearly Meeting House.

Courtesy of the Wayne County Historical Museum, Richmond, Indiana

Once each year, at the mellow season of late autumn, when the harvests had been safely gathered and the men were free for a fortnight, they came, filling our little city with their soberly garbed figures, and filling the great Yearly Meeting-house—as big as the Metropolitan Opera-House—morning, afternoon, and nights, with throngs which came and sat and departed in a silence and composure impossible to believe. There may have been for an hour in the vast barn of a place no stir save the lazy buzzing of a fly high up against a window or the gentle nodding of the oak (calculated to be a thousand years old) seen through the unpainted glass, when Esther Frame or Robert Douglas or some other celebrated Friend would rise and break forth in a rhapsody of spiritual exaltation. There would be no movement when the high voice, sustained to the end like a chant, without an amen died away; none until presently the Friend "at the head of the meeting" extended his hand to his nearest neighbor, and the meeting took a deep breath and "rose."

The National Road was really built, according to the settled belief of my grandmother, Ann Harlan, in order to enable the Friends of Clinton County, Ohio, to come to Yearly Meeting at Richmond. To be sure, the histories talk of other purposes—of a large scheme of internal improvements conceived by Adams and championed by Henry Clay, of the necessity of a military road to the Mexican frontier.

My grandmother takes no stock in such talk. She understands thoroughly that that rough but God-fearing man Andrew Jackson understood the needs of the Friends who had come up from North Carolina in the early years of the nineteenth century. She had always been thankful to Andrew Jackson as she was to Providence for all such things as it is the duty of Providence and Presidents to provide for the righteous, and she travels the National Pike back and forth every year—she has made the journey more than seventy times—to Whitewater Yearly Meeting, with an undisturbed conscience of her own, and a tranquil trust in the goodness of all men and of the workings of all God's world.

Grandmother Harlan's path through life must have been, to judge from the undeviating serenity of her countenance and the never-disturbed equanimity of her soul, as smooth as the surface of the pike, and nothing could be smoother than that. She had faced the Indians as a girl, she had brought up eleven children in the nurture and admonition of the Lord, she had maintained a station of the "Underground Railway" for runaway slaves, and she had seen some of her sons go to the war of slavery, as she always called it; she had buried two husbands and she had had upon her shoulders the trials and troubles of a nation of grandchildren, but her face was as smooth and pink as the face of a child. Always in silk, albeit of sober hue and unchanging cut, with her handkerchief across her breast and her starched cap on her head, Grandmother Harlan was a great lady in her way, though she used to shame us much when she said "cowcumber" or "chimbley."

* * *

It was dusk when I reached the old house—too dark to have seen much in the drive from the station. After dinner we sat on the piazza. The talk was of the changes of twenty years; they were many.

"The stone posts are very handsome, Tom," I said. "They add dignity to the place. There used to hang there one of those long gates with an attachment which tilted it so that it swung open and shut automatically when a wheel struck a sort of outrigger."

"Yes, I recollect," said Tom. "Queer device. Very popular, though, quarter of a century ago."

"The old road is still there, however," I observed.

"Yes; that is an institution which there is no prospect of doing away with."

"Isn't it Yearly Meeting week? I don't suppose any of the Clinton County connection are coming?" I remarked.

"Oh, yes," replied Tom; "indeed they are. Grandmother Harlan never misses. She and Uncle Eli are on the way. What's more, they are due here now. Coming overland, you know, as usual [by horse and buggy]. Couldn't induce Grandmother to travel to Yearly Meeting by rail."

Bless her! Grandmother Harlan coming once more by the old road. That was the best of news. And, indeed, it was Fourth-day night and about the hour at which, I remembered well, the tired grays used to pull in after their long day on the road. This was an ideal return to boyhood's home.

"Yes, they are due almost any minute now," said Tom, studying his watch by the coal of his cigar. "Grandmother, for all her ninety years, is as punctual as the clock."

A sudden light burst out at the top of Linden Hill, dazzling, fiercely powerful, the search-light of something swooping down the road. As it reached the gate, it hesitated, it turned, and, gathering speed again, drew swiftly up to the door—*a panting, six-cylinder motor-car, bringing Grandmother Harlan in huge automobile coat and goggles!*

She explained calmly as she stepped out, her poke-bonnet in her hand:

"Thee knows it was so warm and dusty we did not start till near sundown. Eli thought we could do it nicely in two hours; it is only seventy miles. I should like to have been in time to attend Fourth-day evening meeting. And so we should have been, the Lord willing, but as we went through Bellbrook, —does thee mind the place, William? Thy mother knew it well when she was a little girl—a sparkplug burned out, and the cylinders backfired. I fear Eli was sore beset, for his words were not those of soberness as he tried the cylinders. I said to him, 'Eli, let thy communication be, Yea, yea! Nay, nay.' But he answered, 'Mother, thee knows the Scriptures, but thee knows nothing about a buzz-box.'"

"But, Grandmother," I gasped as soon as I could fairly comprehend the thing, "isn't it unusual for Friends to come to meetings in automobiles? Horses were good enough in the old days."

"William," said Grandmother Harlan, turning on me her gentle eye, and proffering a peppermint, "thee remembers that the Good Book says, 'A horse is a vain thing for safety.'"

And the amazing lady, who had made her first journeys to Yearly Meeting in the saddle, and who had waited nearly a century to incorporate this particular Scripture into her body of doctrine, pressed it home upon me with the look and tone of one uttering a precious, saving truth.

"Besides," continued Grandmother Harlan, laying her small hand upon the tonneau of the vibrating monster—just as, without doubt, standing on the upping-block at this very spot seventy years ago, she had laid it on the neck of the animal that had brought her over—"besides," said Grandmother Harlan, with a last pat for the automobile, "thee knows, William, that no vehicle is so well adapted to the old National Road."

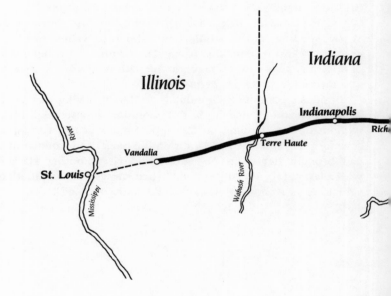

VII. THE MODERN AGE
BRINGS A MODERN ROAD

From seldom-used byway of the past
to U.S. Route 40

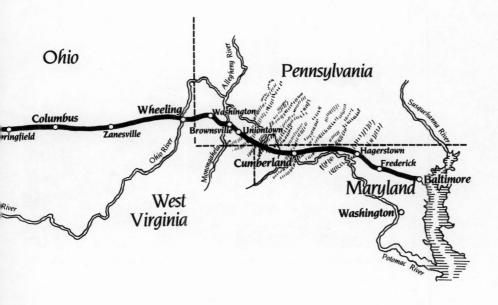

The vanguard of the new era came down the road riding bicycles.

U.S. Bureau of Public Roads (National Archives)

THE ROAD TO "GOOD ROADS"

"They talk much nowadays of good roads," wrote William Bayard Hale. "The idea has even become a movement."

And for good reason. There weren't many roads, or sections of roads, good enough to swoop along. More common in Hale's day was the panting, vibrating monster that got bogged down in some quagmire or broke down traversing some canyon-like crevice. And yet, paradoxically, it was not the automobile that got the modern highway system going; the vanguard of the new came down the road riding bicycles.

It was in the mid-1880s, a decade before the motorcar, that the bicycle in modern form arrived—the "safety" bicycle with low wheels, as it looks today, replacing the high-wheeled veloci-pede of quaint looks and unstable disposition. The safety was at first a plaything of the rich, but with mass production it quickly became a reasonably cheap, reliable, and safe form of transpor-tation for rich or poor, city or country dweller. But where to ride the safety safely? It wasn't a question of traffic; automobiles were a precious few, and horses were apt to be afraid enough of the bicyclist that some local ordinances required the cyclist to dismount when approaching the horse. The hindrance to cy-cling was the deplorable condition of the roads.

What came to be known as the Good Roads Movement was spearheaded by bicyclists organizing themselves into local clubs and, on a broader basis, the League of American Wheelmen, all working for improved roads. But the cyclists were only the start of it. Farmers joined in, for the economics of farming had changed. Heretofore, farms were close to population centers; now, after the turn of the century, the growth of cities meant greater distance between farm and market and thus another impetus to improved roads. And even the railroads could support the Good Roads Movement: Feeder roads for automobiles would bring new riders to trunk-line railroads.

The result in 1893 was creation of the Office of Road Inquiry in the U.S. Department of Agriculture—a federal agency to collect data, answer questions from local authorities, and encourage development of improved roads on the part of local, county, and state governments. It was the closest the federal government had come to taking responsibility for roads since the Cumberland Road Act almost a century earlier. Though it was hardly imagined that the Office of Road Inquiry would ever help finance road construction, let alone build a road, it was the embryo of all federal aid for road building in future years.

* * *

Meanwhile, the automobile had arrived in the 1890s, demonstrating even more dramatically than the bicycle the need for good roads. One holder of a seat of power who understood the political economics of federal aid to roads and who also knew firsthand what it was like ride them was Congressman Albert Douglas of Ohio, who, in 1909, decided to drive his new Model-T Ford home from Washington over what was left of the old National Road rather than have the car shipped by rail.

A good-roads advocate, Robert Bruce, writing in *Motor* magazine four years later, saw "the old national highway" only awaiting "a magic touch" to make it a superhighway of the future—and the prototype for a new whole new network of roads nationwide.

ALBERT DOUGLAS, 1909
By Model-T Ford, Frederick to Zanesville

Albert Douglas
Library of Congress

When the extra session of the 61st Congress adjourned on the 5th of August, we had bought our railroad tickets, reserved berths in the sleeping car and expected to proceed home to Chillicothe by the conventional railroad train; but when I suggested to my wife [Lucia] that instead of shipping our motor car we should ride home in it over the old National Road she readily agreed.

So the next day at noon, with our driver at the wheel and our light luggage by his side, we started from our Washington abode and took the Seventh Street pike right north out of the city for Olney and Ridgeville, Md., where we were to strike the old road.

One of Betsy's brethren—a 1909 Model-T Ford, complete with Ohio license plate.

Smithsonian Institution Photo No. 49962

"At the summit of Big Savage, we caught a glorious view of meadows, fields, woods, and piled up mountains."—Albert Douglas

Today that same view—including Rt. 40-48, a superhighway. The photograph was taken from old Rt. 40, the National Road, at the summit of Big Savage.

A couple of hours brought us to Ridgeville and then, after a good dinner at "The Eagle," a roadhouse well known to local tourists, we started over the famous old Pike towards the setting sun. "Betsy," as we familiarly call our little Ford machine, was in good humor, and though the road was hilly and somewhat rough we reached Frederick, fourteen miles away, before four o'clock.

The road from Frederick to Hagerstown, crossing the Catoctin and South mountains, was familiar to us as we had passed over it on former visits to the battlefields of Antietam and Gettysburg; but the road itself is good, the country through which it passes is beautiful as well as full of historic interest, and the afternoon ride was most enjoyable.

From Hagerstown to Cold Spring the road is made of blue limestone, crushed and machine-rolled, so that it is about as smooth and hard as concrete. The evening ride with the great ridges of the Alleghanies before us looming up in the light of the sinking sun was most enjoyable; so that when a half hour's ride brought us to the pretty village of Cold Spring we decided to go on to Hancock. It was after leaving Cold Spring that our real mountain ride began, for we had to climb several long ridges on the "low speed," and it was after eight o'clock when we reached Hancock, the speedometer registering 103.5 miles.

The less said about the Maryland-Inn at Hancock, the better and we were not sorry to leave betimes in the morning. "Betsy" had received a satisfactory breakfast of oil and gasoline and seemed glad to be off. A motor car comes with familiar use to have a sort of personal character and it seems in no-wise out of place to speak of her "humor," as one would of any human thing. Her temper was sorely tried however before she reached the friendly shelter of the garage at Cumberland shortly before noon, for she had a rough road to travel, and up and down five great ridges of that system of mountains we call Appalachian.

The machine growled up the long rocky ridges on the "low gear," and sometimes, as we were in no haste to catch a train or "make" any particular point by a fixed hour, she would stop a bit, not to rest but to let the boiling water in her tank cool a little. Then the wife and I would get down and walk on ahead, picking the blackberries ripening on every hand, gathering flowers or drinking from some of the many roadside springs, walled and protected so well by the wagoners in other days that they still furnish cool and attractive places to rest and drink.

The telephone companies have taken advantage of the direct and convenient route of the National Road to erect their lines, and for the whole way through Maryland, Virginia and West

Virginia to Wheeling, three systems of poles and wires follow the pike.

At "Fort" Cumberland we were met by a hospitable friend and after a pleasant visit of two hours including luncheon, he accompanied us on our way as far as Frostburg, returning by the trolley line. At Frostburg our crossing of the Alleghanies really began, only to end at Somerfield at the "Big Crossings," the name given by the wagoners and stagemen to the three sturdy stone arches which form the bridge over the Youghiogheny, and which, completed as its tablet testifies on July 4th, 1818, still stands seemingly as secure as ever.

The intervening ridges bear quaint names: Big Savage, Little Savage, Red Hill or the Shades-of-Death, Little Meadow, Negro Mountain, Keyser Ridge, and Winding Ridge.

We found the road up Big Savage, a grade of about 1,800 feet in two miles, one of the worst on the whole trip, and a disgrace to whomsoever may be responsible for its condition. For this there might be some excuse if it were comparatively unused, but on the contrary we found it on that Saturday afternoon thronged with teams. The stones out of which the old road was constructed, lay loosened amid the sand and dust, and through them "Betsy" had to fairly plow her way. The sun was hot too and that half hour was the only one approaching discomfort on our long ride. But when we came to the summit, and caught the glorious view to the West and Southwest, of meadows, fields, woods, and piled up mountains, our discomfort vanished and there followed a long afternoon of unalloyed pleasure; up hill and down, through forests and mountain farms, meadows and pastures, fields of blooming buckwheat, the prettiest crop the farmer grows. The air was cool and invigorating and the view both West and East superb.

Passing the crest of Winding Ridge we began the long slope down towards the "crossings" of the Youghiogheny. Part of the road here had been newly repaired with crushed and rolled limestone, and we flew over it towards the fast setting sun through pretty, well kept villages filled with summer boarders, past beautiful homes with close clipped lawns, beautiful gardens and handsome buildings and through well cared for meadows and farm lands, until we crossed the river on its historic bridge at Somerfield, called "Smithfield" on the mile-posts.

Shortly after sundown we drew up with sounding horn in front of the attractive looking hotel on Chalk Hill, only to find every room taken and nothing to do but to push on to Uniontown some ten miles further. However our lamps were soon lighted, the road was good, the evening fine and by eight o'clock we had passed the Summit House on Laurel Ridge, a

A reminder of the past: the Old Pike Restaurant in Claysville,
Pennsylvania.

favorite resort for the people of Uniontown, down the long four mile grade, past the romantic glen called "Turkey's Nest," and past gleaming rows of coke-ovens on the opposite hillsides, into the city of Uniontown and into the very excellent hotel kept by a Mr. Tetlow and bearing his name. We did full justice to the good supper served us and to the excellent "room with a bath, please," to which we were shown.

We woke to another fine morning, and at nine o'clock bowled out, through the "West End" of Uniontown, with the top of the machine down and the sun once more behind us. Our way this day lay through Brownsville and Washington to Wheeling, and then over the river once more into that part of the "Northwest Territory" allotted by Congress in 1802 to "Ohio." The country was rolling and beautiful, but we missed the hills and woods and looked back with regret to the misty mountain tops.

At Washington we visited the buildings and campus of the Washington and Jefferson college, gave "Betsy" a drink of gasoline and telephoned ahead to Claysville for luncheon to be ready in an hour. But that lunch had to wait, for by some unaccountable mischance we took the wrong turning somewhere between Washington and Claysville and spent an extra hour finding our way across the country. After all the luncheon was not very good anyhow even if the town was named for "Harry of the West." Two miles west of Claysville the road ascends one of its longest and steepest hills to West Alexander and from this village to Wheeling the road is fine with a steady decent of about twelve miles.

Just as it was five P.M. when we reached the top of the Alleghanies, so by chance it was exactly twenty-four hours later that we rolled upon the great suspension bridge at Wheeling, paid our two tolls and crossed over Jordan into the promised land [his home state of Ohio].

We passed the night in a little roadside inn at Hendrysburg, near the borders of Guernsey and Belmont, made our third and last morning's start at seven o'clock, passed Cambridge at nine, and into Zanesville before eleven. After rest and refreshment we left Zanesville and the National Road at one o'clock and travelling over the route of the old "Zanesville and Maysville Turnpike" arrived at Chillicothe at six, without a single serious mishap or detention, and after a most enjoyable and informing journey.

The National Road today as a way of travel may be described by the old phrase, "good, bad and indifferent." In spots it is excellent, and in spots it is execrable. But its most serious defect and discomfort for motoring are the bumps, breakers or "thank-you-marms" on every hill, no matter what the grade.

Modern road-making of course knows them not; and in the old specifications of the government engineering department for repairing the road as far back as 1832, I find this language: "At proper intervals on the slopes of hills, drains or catch-waters (they seem to have had the same trouble then as now giving the things a name) must be made across the road.... These catch-waters must be made with a gradual curvature so as to give no jolts to the wheels of carriages passing over them." But the "gradual curvature" is omitted now-a-days and the jolts are there. As the years pass and "horseless carriages" become as common as horses, and pleasant travel by private conveyances increases, we may expect to see the roads repaired by modern methods and "catch-waters" will no more vex and delay the traveller.

With all of these changing conditions who can say what the future history of this famous old National Pike may be? Our children may see its glories revive, its way repaved with modern metal, its broken and defaced old mile-posts repaired or replaced, its toll houses rebuilt or re-occupied, its iron gates once more threatening the "joy-rider," [but] its sides lined with colossal advertising signs, darkening the view, and its old taverns renovated, rebuilt, re-established—but with "soft drinks" perhaps substituted for the "fifteen-cent-a-gallon" [whiskey] of other days. Who can tell! But in any event to fond students of the past, to men who love to revive in imagination the days of the pioneers and to dwell in thought among the days that are no more, the romance of this old pathway of the nation will live forever.

ROBERT BRUCE, 1913
Writing in Motor *Magazine*

Except for short pieces of road in National Cemeteries, Army Posts, National Parks and the like, the Federal Government [long ago] gave up all highway construction, and has never resumed it on this continent. The final appropriation was on June 17, 1844, when a supplementary bill was passed [in Congress] carrying $1,359.81 for "arrearages," and the accounts of the Old National Road were closed after a total expenditure of $6,824,919.33—a large sum in those days; but without question, for every dollar spent in the building and maintenance of this road, ten dollars were added to the wealth of the territories it traversed, and thereby to the nation.

No other highway in America was ever built so straight for

From *Motor Magazine,* March 1913: an illustration accompanying Robert Bruce's article and dramatizing the condition of the National Road at the beginning of the age of the automobile. The photograph was taken on the eastern slope of Polish Mountain, east of Cumberland, Maryland. The caption reads: "A view of the National Highway at its worst, which motorists will agree, is bad enough."

such long distances, or is now so free from steep grades or dangerous curves. "Riding by night," says a Pittsburg motorist, "the polar star hangs persistently in the same general direction mile after mile; sometimes four or five ascents and descents can be seen ahead or behind, but usually all in a straight line." Road engineers find its location today practically beyond criticism throughout.

While the surface of the road has been worn away in many sections, the foundation work is unusually good. There were always many waterbars on the National Road, but they are growing less, and will be done away with altogether, as new methods entirely take the place of the old.

Taking up present conditions on different sections of this great natural thoroughfare between the East and the West, we find the worst obstacles of all between Hagerstown and Cumberland in Maryland, which is particularly unfortunate, because it handicaps tourist travel desirous of reaching points on the old road from either the East or the South. Competent observers state that parts of this stretch are in worse condition than they were five years ago, which is certainly not complimentary to Maryland.

The only hope for the improvement of this vital stretch (aside from Federal aid, which is not likely to be undertaken right away), is in Maryland; and in answer to a recent inquiry, O.E. Weller, Chairman of the State Roads Commission, Baltimore, says that it is the purpose of the Commission to improve the Frederick Turnpike, and the Old National Road through Maryland at the earliest possible moment. Unfortunately, however, under the present Maryland law, the money raised for building State roads is allotted among the twenty-three counties on the basis of county mileage, instead of on the mileage of State roads necessary to complete the improvements demanded by the heavy through travel. No more inconvenient or unsatisfactory system could be devised, and as a result there are gaps or uncompleted links in the State road system, especially in the several western counties, through which the National Highway passes.

That part of the old Turnpike in Pennsylvania is not only in better condition now than the Maryland end, but it is already faring better in the way of improvements; several stretches have lately been resurfaced.

Between Wheeling and Columbus the National Highway is practically straight through Cambridge and Zanesville; most of the travel goes that way without serious inconvenience, despite the rough surface and the frequent hills. From Columbus to Springfield, Ohio, and thence to Richmond, Ind., and on to

Indianapolis, there is practically no other route than the National Road, or any real need of any, as the foundation is solid, the surface fair, and bridges and culverts are in good condition throughout. This is today by far the best long stretch between Baltimore and St. Louis. Meanwhile, the section from Terre Haute to St. Louis is passable, though admittedly bad in spots, especially in wet weather, when the drains are often stopped up and the roadbed is full of mud holes.

There is no doubt whatever that the present great advancement in road improvement throughout the country will shortly redeem the old national highway, which is simply waiting for the magic touch that will bring back its old-time importance, except that pleasure travel will take the place of the stage coaches and the freight wagons.

ROADS CALLED "NATIONAL" ONCE AGAIN

Even as "Betsy" was completing that long haul from Washington to Chillicothe, the notion that the automobile could travel longer hauls—even go from coast to coast—was no longer a flight of fancy. Before the turn of the century, auto builder Alexander Winton had driven one of his cars from Cleveland to New York in ten days, and in 1903 three drivers made news by going cross-country in only fifty-three days.

But that was by a hodgepodge of roads. Why not a coast-to-coast highway—one single route—using existing roads where possible, improving them or building new where necessary. One such route, which came to be known as the Lincoln Highway, was first proposed in 1912 by Carl G. Fisher, an Indianapolis businessman, and taken up and promoted by automobile manufacturers. Undertaken at the outset in 1914 with $4 million in private contributions, it later received federal funding, and it cost about $90 million when eventually completed in the mid-1920s from New Jersey to California—some 3,400 miles. It became U.S. Route 30. And then other routes were proposed: the Missouri Old Trails Association urging a cross-country National Old Trails Road that included the old National Road, which largely became U.S. Route 40. Still other highways promoted by private commercial interests included the Dixie Highway, the Atlantic Pacific Highway, and the Old Spanish Trail. And how to make these routes easy to follow? Much the same as Nemacolin had done at the behest of Thomas Cresap in making a multiplicity of trails tangible as one through the wilderness: with markings—in this case, colored bands affixed to telephone poles along the way, different colors and designs designating different routes.

Motorists' guides were also steering drivers along scenic and historic routes. *The Official Automobile Blue Book of 1914,* for example, gave automobilists a detailed guide to following the old National Road, often advising that it was best to follow the tracks of the trolleys that had proliferated in the 1890s and early years of the twentieth century: "Go under RRs. following trolley"; "Pick up trolley tracks on E. Maiden St."; "turn left with trolley into 12th St." The *Blue Book* of 1914 found the old road generally in good shape, as in this brief introduction to a tour of the road between Cumberland and Wheeling: "Via Uniontown, Beallsville and Washington. The old National Pike, some good macadam and pike. Undergoing repairs 1912 and 1913, and in excellent condition 1914. Fine scenery from mountains. This route along the old National Turnpike has been greatly improved and is easily followed."

The federal government was now going beyond mere exchange of road-building information. With the Post Office Appropriation Act of 1912, it made available federal aid for roads (nominally post roads) for the first time. The appropriation was $500,000, and required that a participating state or local subdivision spend $2 for each $1 of federal aid received; but only 13 states and 28 counties took advantage, and only 455 miles of road were built. What is most fitting is that the first grant was for none other than the National Road—rebuilding of a 50-mile stretch between Columbus and Zanesville. Four years later, with the Rural Post Road Act of 1916, funding increased to $75 million over a five-year period, on a fifty-fifty matching basis. Moreover, the Office of Road Inquiry was now the Office of Public Roads.

A year after this landmark legislation, America's entry into World War I demonstrated further the necessity of a national road network. The railroads of the time could not handle the increased volume of passengers and matériel. Freight cars backed up on sidings, creating massive backlogs. The Council for National Defense recommended that trucks bound for Europe, instead of being shipped by rail, travel on their own power from Detroit and other Midwestern manufacturing centers, carrying matériel of war with them. The first convoy of thirty trucks, of which twenty-nine reached their destination, left Detroit December 17, 1917, making the trip to Baltimore in part over the old National Road. Convoy after convoy followed.

The war over, it was clear that a federally funded national highway system would have to be a peacetime priority. The

The west side of Sideling Hill near Hancock, Maryland, ca. 1910.

The approximate site today. At this point Rt. 40-Alt., the old road, is one and the same with Rt. 40-48, a limited-access superhighway.

"No other highway in America was ever built so straight for such long distances."—Robert Bruce

U.S. 40 east of Grantsville, Maryland, 1934. Although other highways with long straight stretches were abuilding, the National Road's unprecedented straightness was still a marvel into the twentieth century. Note white paint on utility poles as aid to night driving.

U.S. Bureau of Public Roads (National Archives)

Despite its many long straight stretches, the National Road had its curves, especially into and out of the S-bridges that remained in use in the early days of motoring. Thus the warning to motorists to sound their klaxon horns and drive slowly. This sign, identified only as being in Muskingum County, Ohio, was almost certainly at the approach to one of the S-bridges at New Concord.

National Archives

Sunday drivers still had the road to themselves in this photograph, taken on a Sunday afternoon in 1916 in Liking County, Ohio. Yet it was estimated that only two vehicles in a hundred, at this time, were still horse-drawn.

U.S. Bureau of Public Roads (National Archives)

Reminiscent of the ceremony at Belmont County, as the National Road began its journey through Ohio in 1825, were the civic ceremonies of 1925-26 when ribbon cuttings and oratory helped to welcome new federal highways throughout the land.

New Concord, Ohio: Rededication of an old National Road bridge as part of U.S. 40, ca. 1925.

What was left of the old National Road in the mid-1920s became part of U.S. 40, one of the first of the new federal-aid primary routes created by the Federal Highway Act of 1921.

U.S. Bureau of Public Roads (National Archives)

Federal Highway Act of 1921 sought to do that through an established program of federal aid that would encourage the states to build "an adequate and connected system of highways, interstate in character." Within two years this had evolved into the federal-aid primary highway system (the U.S. 40s and the like)—with its systematic numbering of interconnecting highways, even numbers going east-west and odd numbers north-south—totaling some 169,000 miles (out of 3 million miles of roads throughout the country, carrying nearly 20 million cars and trucks in 1925). It was welcomed, wherever it went, with the same sense of community pride that had greeted the National Road in its day. Reminiscent of the ceremony at the Belmont County Courthouse, with its reading of the Declaration of Independence and volley of rifle fire as the National Road began its journey through Ohio in 1825, were the civic ceremonies of 1925–26—ribbon cuttings and oratory welcoming the new federal highways throughout the land. Among the first roads to be significantly improved and so designated with shield-shaped signs placed at intervals along the way was this same National Road, now a part of U.S. Route 40, a true "national" road from coast to coast.

* * *

In its new life, the old road thrived. A traveler in the 1940s could find it "busier than in all its 140 years...looking confidently ahead to a future as thrilling as its romantic past." This particular traveler was Philip Jordan, a professor of American history, surveying the old road in part through the eyes of a trucker—a John Deets or Jesse Piersol of the twentieth century.

PHILIP JORDAN, 1947
By Automobile and Tractor-Trailer Truck, Columbus to Cumberland

U.S. 40 never sleeps. Its branches from Washington, D.C., and Baltimore funnel thousands of passenger cars and trucks through prosperous, modern Cumberland, over the Alleghanies and through a Middle Western heartland to St. Louis and beyond. At no time in the National Road's long life of more than 140 years has it been busier.

Automatic traffic signals, blinking red, amber and green, guard today's intersections. Yellow lines divide pavement, warning drivers to stay on their own side of the road. The narrow road of the 1920's has widened to three, and even four, lanes. Wire cables guard drop-offs. The motorist finds blind curves

Philip Jordan in 1946.

Courtesy of the University of Minnesota Archives

eradicated. Scores of signs—"Don't Pass On Hills," "Don't Cross Yellow Line," "Cattle Crossing"—help to make today's driving safe. State highway departments send blunt-nosed snowplows to clear the road in winter and cumbersome cement mixers to repair holes after the spring thaw. The road is tended like a baby. In the old days its sides and banks eroded and slipped, a constant hazard to stagecoaching. Today, banks are landscaped, picnic tables erected and garbage cans provided. The early nineteenth-century traveler drank from any roadside spring he passed. The modern driver sees ahead, as he flashes along: "Pure drinking water—500 feet."

The road is lined with new taverns, some doing business where Jacksonian inns stood. Many attempt to recreate the old days with parlors filled with antique cherry tables and walnut rocking chairs. But the bar alcove with its array of squat bottles is gone. The pewter castor has disappeared from the dining room, and the hitching rack and boot scraper have been destroyed. Waitresses in nylons and starched uniforms have replaced the cotton-stockinged, calico-clad maids of 100 years ago. And short orders are more in demand than leisurely dinners. Tourists are always in a hurry. They slap their coins on a counter near the cigar stand and are off to do another 200 miles before dark. The old road has become a hurried, neurotic highway. Tens of thousands of automobiles pass a given point on it annually. Horns blare and tires squeak. Drivers want to get where they are going in a hurry.

U.S. 40 is a work road and a hauling route as well as a pleasant thoroughfare for swift-running passenger cars. The trucker has replaced the romantic wagoner with his six-horse team and eight-ton freight schooner. As picturesque as his predecessor, the jehu of a mighty "semi" is the king of drivers. He has his own trade traits, his own vocabulary and his own peculiar superstitions. In his cab he possesses the authority of a captain on the bridge of his ship.

Thompson Derby, lean and short-spoken, started pushing a truck over the National Road before World War II. Liking the freight business, he grabbed the first chance he got in the Army to slide behind the wheel of a military van. His job was hauling supplies in Italy. Derby drove mostly at night, without lights, but he was accustomed to night driving. Most trucking in peacetime is done at night, when highways are relatively clear of passenger cars. Then too, goods ordered one day may be shipped that evening and, as a result of all-night driving, be delivered the next morning.

On the job [in Columbus], Derby picked up Dailey Jackson, his assistant, at four in the afternoon and drove to the dock, a

"Derby and Jackson 'spelled' each other driving an International K-8, a heavy-duty, truck-tractor with a van-type semitrailer."

A 1940s International tractor-trailer, photographed in Baltimore.

Library of Congress (Photograph by John Vachon)

great yard filled with trucks. Derby's semitrailer was bigger than anything he had piloted before he went into the service. Derby got his orders and bills of lading from the dock office and swung into the cab. Jackson climbed up beside him. Engine heat came up in great waves. Gears meshed and air brakes grumbled, a peculiar noise midway between a drawn-out s-w-i-s-h and a sharp hiss. They edged out of the terminal dock.

By this time twilight interfered with visibility. Derby drove cautiously, selecting side streets where Columbus traffic was not dense and where he could travel at a steady rate. Twenty miles east of town Derby angled off the highway to pull up before a low frame building with a neon blinker that spelled out "EATS." It was today's version of yesterday's wagoners' inn.

The National Highway at night is a procession of trucks, their bright lights a variegated stream of color. Grumbling and growling, they labor in low gear up steep grades and ease off for gentle slopes. Motorists, sleeping in tourist homes, complain of the noise and swear that next time they'll find a place away from the highway. But modern freight ways cannot stop because tourists damn the noisy twentieth-century wagoner.

Derby, swinging along through Zanesville, knew he was making no more racket than necessary. He went through towns as quietly as possible and was careful to watch his speed. In one or two communities local constables deliberately preyed on truckers.

Derby pulled off the road, shook Jackson awake and had a cigarette. When the semitrailer got under way, Jackson was driving. Now the responsibility for delivering safely thousands of pounds of cash registers, electric freezers, dry goods and office furniture was his. He clicked off his bright headlights about the time Wheeling loomed ahead.

After picking up a ton and a half at Wheeling, Derby swung from the terminal up Wheeling Hill and headed for Brownsville. A horn blared, and he moved over to let a small van by. A film-delivery truck, lined with steel, scooted past with tomorrow's motion pictures. Two short toots, and again Derby veered to the right. A Greyhound bus, bound for Washington by way of Baltimore, thundered by.

Derby and Jackson "spelled" each other with the driving every 100 miles. They stopped frequently through the Alleghenies, getting out for short walks to take the kinks out of their legs and give the engine a chance to cool. Driving an International K-8, a heavy-duty, truck-tractor with a van-type semitrailer, over Savage Mountain was no easy task for Derby when he first returned from Italy. But he had grown used to it. Now he knew every twist and turn of the National Road.

He wheeled through Granstville and Frostburg and on into

Cumberland. There he unloaded. A telegram from Columbus was waiting for him. It said to go to Baltimore, pick up a load from Washington and get his next orders at the terminal there.

Thoroughly modernized, Uncle Sam's old pike looks confidently ahead to a future as thrilling as its romantic past. Old-timers, horse-and-buggy pioneers, say that the flavor of the road is gone; that improved roads and modern automobiles have made U.S. 40 much like any other American highway. Yet chamber of commerce secretaries state flatly that the National Road is different from other roads. "History was made along this trail," they say. "Thousands travel it annually just because it is the country's most historic national highway." The road's admirers scorn skeptics who predict that the new Pennsylvania turnpike will divert traffic from the National Road and eventually reduce U.S. 40 to an unimportant east-west thoroughfare. "It's always been there and always will be," they say.

At night mighty giants of the sky, motors thundering and green and red lights gleaming, set their course by twinkling air beacons that parallel U.S. 40. Friends of Uncle Sam's highway point up. "See, even air liners follow the Cumberland Road."

THE OLD ROAD AND THE NEW

Not all that was new in transportation was thundering overhead. Highway travel was still changing. Whereas U.S. 40 had evolved primarily out of existing roads, an entirely new road system was taking shape that would carve many new routes through the land. It had already been started in 1941, with federal legislation creating a 7,500-mile system of national defense highways, but relatively few miles were completed after the outbreak of World War II. In 1944, Congress expanded the concept to an interstate system for peacetime as well as for defense, but there continued to be little progress until the Federal-Aid Highway Act of 1956, which effectively created the Interstate highway system as it is known today. What gave incentive to a vast increase in construction was that the federal government now pledged 90 percent of the cost—a notable change from the original fifty-fifty arrangement instituted for federal-aid primary highways. By the late 1980s, the Interstate system totaled more than 44,000 miles, built at a cost of more than $100 billion. (The federal-aid primary routes—the Route 40s of the country— meanwhile totaled more than 301,000 miles.)

The limited-access interstates, now clearly the fastest and safest highways in the land, divert traffic from the old routes

*wherever they parallel one another. For long-distance travel,
the Interstates have a clear edge in comfort and speed, as well
as safety engineering, and are clearly the more heavily traveled.
Except where there is no alternative Interstate route, the older
federal-aid primary routes are used more for local and intrastate
travel.*

* * *

*Our final traveler is the author himself, his account based on
notes of trips over the old National Road in 1988 and 1989.*

MERRITT IERLEY, 1989

By 1988 Nova Hatchback, Baltimore to Vandalia

This thread of earth respun by time and now become a cord of
concrete ... this "splendid highway that fulfilled the tide of
civilization" ... this "grand national road" ...

What is it like in a grand new era of transportation? In the
company of those who have gone this way before, let us travel
again this great avenue of history, and see.

To begin ... where else? Where the turnpike builders began in
1797. In Baltimore. Using U.S. 40, we can follow the approximate route of the old road, but now it is a divided, four-lane
superhighway. There is absolutely nothing to see of the old—
surely nothing of the country-like road that in the 1860s wound
about through Waverly Terrace, now part of the urban canyon
through which new 40 throbs. This is a down-to-business
highway that speeds us through the city and its suburbs and
hurls us into the Maryland countryside.

A truck stop outside of Frederick, known as Truck City,
quintessentially twentieth-century though it is, would be recog-
nizable to John Deets or Jesse Piersol. The conveyances have
changed—they're 400-horse diesels now instead of 10-horse
Conestogas—but the logistics are basically the same: Both kinds
of rigs need a lot wagon yard; and their wagoners, a lot of good
food and comfortable bunks. Jesse remembered sitting on a
bucket turned bottom-up at a wagon stand of old, listening to a
hundred horses grinding corn. He should hear fifty or a hundred trucks idling—their diesel engines gurgling and snorting,
their refrigeration units whining.

West of Hagerstown, we leave the Piedmont plateau and
begin our ascent into the Alleghenies. For much of the way

The author as photographer, with 1988 Nova Hatchback used for trips
on the National Road.

Photograph by Gretchen Bock

An old-timer who likes to reminisce, Arthur White

"An old stager."

Harper's Magazine, November 1879

along this stretch, U.S. 40 either closely parallels or is one and the same as Interstate 70 and there's nothing at all to remind us of the old road. The mountain scenery is indeed spectacular, though the more widely traveled tourist of today would be less likely than William Rideing or Rufus Wilson to see it "rivaling in beauty and grandeur the noblest passes of the Sierras."

Rideing found a couple of old-timers who liked to reminisce. Hancock today has its Arthur White, eightyish and a dweller of the old road for the better part of this century. His home is on what is now West Main (wherever the National Road isn't called National anymore, it's most likely known as Main Street), across the street from the variety store his father and mother bought in 1919. At the corner there once stood a large historical sign proclaiming that this was at one time known as the Bank Road—a section of the National Pike so called for the Baltimore bankers who built it. "It was a nice big metal sign," recalls White nostalgically, "and tourists used to stop and take pictures of it. Then some smartass came and took it down. But it doesn't make much difference now. Most of the traffic is out on the bypass [Interstate 70]. We don't have tourists like we used to."

After Hancock, some 25 miles to the west of Hagerstown, I-70 departs for the north to join the Pennsylvania Turnpike for the trip west toward Wheeling, thence again to parallel U.S. 40 or even rejoin it here and there in Ohio. From Hancock, U.S. 40 pokes through the mountains and continues west along the route of the old National Road through Cumberland. Here it is mostly a modern, four-lane highway, and it is busiest along this section because there is otherwise no highway going through these mountains. In large part, the traffic is trucks—eighteen-wheelers, many of them, charging down one hill to get momentum for the next. There is a "scenic alternate" for a few miles along this route, but remarkably, it is not more scenic. It follows the original alignment of the old road and consequently has a number of tree-lined horseshoe curves that restrict the view, whereas the new U.S. 40 along here is more of a superhighway, and hence, being more open and straight, allows for a greater spectacle of hills turning into mountains.

Cumberland, a city proud of its history, has commemorative markers all over the place, especially where Fort Cumberland used to be, but the only extant reminder of the fort is a cabin built in 1755 for a newly appointed colonel named George Washington. It looks as it did then, but were Washington to return today he would surely be amazed. The cabin talks. Actually, of course, it is a concealed tape recorder with external speaker that, when asked by the push of a button, recounts its history to passers-by.

The original Cumberland Road proceeded almost due west from here, following the trail laid down by Indian hunters. Today it's Greene Street, house-lined on either side; and yet, not exactly another city street. It's narrower than most, and its gentle windings give suspicion to its aboriginality. This trail was the most direct route to the west, over Haystack Mountain. But what was direct and practical for horses and riders in single file was not the most practical for the wagons and coaches of later travelers. Hence the "new" route, a considerably more level if more roundabout road through The Narrows.

The Narrows has often been called the "Gateway to the West," forming, as it does, a natural passageway through two massive slopes of the Alleghenies. Impressive as it is today, it must have been awesome to the pioneers in the early days of the road—this symbolic as well as actual passage into a new life through the titanic loins of Mother Earth.

This passage (as life) had its exactments. At the 6-mile post there stands, meticulously preserved, a unique, hexagonal structure that no traveler of old could miss, especially because there was a gate across the road. It was the first toll house on the trip west, built in 1833, when the federal government turned this section of the road over to the state. The toll schedule, painstakingly repainted by hand, remains posted—3 cents for a horse and rider, 6 cents for a horse and chaise, 12 cents for a score of driven cattle, and so on. Its modern-day locale of motels ($26 single) and gas stations (93 cents a gallon, regular) also has prices posted.

Since it is the present, we depart toll-free and resume our journey. Frostburg, some 12 miles to the west, with its many fast-food establishments, is still a major stopping place on the road, though there's nothing left of the old taverns or stagecoach stops that were the fast-food places of their day. Nor of the "deer, bears, wolves, wild turkies, and indeed all kinds of wild animals" seen hereabouts by William Blane in 1822.

The climb to Frostburg was only a warmup. Next it's Big Savage Mountain (elevation 2,850 feet). This is where Congressman Douglas's "Betsy" had to "fairly plow her way" up through loosened stones, sand, and dust. The road up Big Savage is a smooth one now, but it's still as formidable a climb. Or descent. A sign at the summit warns trucks going down to stop right there momentarily; then proceed in low gear; then come to a full stop again at intervals, in order not to gain too much momentum. That's how steep it is. One can imagine an early Model-T, going up, veritably chugging its pistons out. Or Captain Orme going down: "its descent is very rugged and almost perpendicular; in passing which we intirely demolished

Andy Jackson at Ben Bean's Tavern in Hancock, Maryland on the way
to his inauguration: "If the president of the United States showed up
today and wanted ham and eggs..."

Harper's Magazine, November 1879

"Its great arch a seeming yawn from out some timeless sleep...like some Roman ruin strangely misplaced."—The Author's Journal

The Casselman River Bridge near Grantsville, Maryland, built in 1813 and in continuous use until 1933.

three waggons and shattered several." Modern road building has
reduced the mountain's propensity for demolition, but there
are only a few trucks of local destination that use Big Savage
now anyway; otherwise they're all down below on a serenely
level stretch of U.S. 40–48, the "National Freeway," a veritable
superhighway that is now a part of the "glorious view of
meadows, fields, woods, and piled up mountains" that Douglas
recorded in his journal at the crest of Big Savage.

Douglas's journal comes to mind a few miles further. "With
all these changing conditions," he wondered in 1909, "who can
say what the future history of this famous old National Pike may
be? Our children may see its glories revived, its way repaved
[but] its sides lined with colossal advertising signs, darkening
the view, and its old taverns renovated, rebuilt . . . but with soft
drinks." Douglas comes to mind once again, out in the rolling
countryside now, as we pass the ruins of an ancient barn built
near the old road but readily observable from now-adjacent U.S.
40–48. One entire side has become colossal: "Exit 34 . . .
5 miles . . . McDonald's."

Another mountain, a few hills, and a few twists of the old
road, and we come upon a sight both expected and yet unexpected. We weren't looking for it at the time. It's where the old
alignment bears off almost imperceptibly to the right while the
new road with a new bridge bears predominantly to the left.
There's an artisans' colony within the fork, occupying a number
of old log cabins, and that catches our eye. We decide to stop.
Then, as we look for a place to park, we see it—its great arch a
seeming yawn from out some timeless sleep. Is it? It has to be.
Or else some ancient Roman ruin strangely misplaced. Yes, this
is it—that "monument of taste and power" that Charles Fenno
Hoffman told us to look for. The great National Road bridge
over the Casselman River, long asleep but bidding us wake it
and be at one with it for a spell. Here . . . is the old road in its
actuality. Not some reconstruction. Not some museum exhibit.
Not some commemorative marker with a talking box. Here is
communion with the road itself, with the very tangible surface
of it. It is deserted and silent, but one can almost hear the
squeal of iron wagon wheel and hollow thud of hoof upon its
ancient stones. One looks across, half expecting to see Andrew
Jackson come galloping by on his way to Washington.

The bridge was in continuous use from 1813 to 1933, when a
new bridge—as patently gangly as the old is gracefully rugged—
was built along a new alignment that parallels the original road
by a few hundred feet. The old was left in place and is now part
of a tiny state park that otherwise includes a few picnic tables
by the side of the Casselman River.

Beyond the bridge there is Keysers Ridge, and then it is only a few miles to the Pennsylvania state line, before crossing which, an observation. Interest in the old road and its colorful heritage, if anything, seems to be resurging. There is now an annual National Pike Festival celebrated along the old road in Pennsylvania and Maryland. The festival is sponsored by county and state agencies working in cooperation with interested private citizens. Each May, it features such activities as wagon trains, entertainment of all sorts, antique car shows, essay contests, and commemorative cancellations at post offices.

Over the Pennsylvania state line, the road takes us past Big Crossings—today following a new alignment over an ordinary, modern, concrete-and-steel bridge spanning the Youghiogheny River. The original stone-arch bridge, once the longest on the old road, is gone. And yet not. If one comes looking most winters, it is there to see. What used to be a narrow river is now the broad Youghiogheny River Lake, a major recreation area created by the damming of the Yough as a flood control measure in the 1940s, leaving the bridge under 50 feet of water. Each summer, and for part of spring and fall, the lake is a place for boating, fishing, and swimming; but in winter, the water level is lowered. If it is dropped far enough, as is usually the case, the old bridge reappears, dries itself off, and, like some giant frog, stretches out in the sun.

(As luck would have it, the summer of 1989 was unusually wet, dictating that the level of the lake not be dropped as much as usual. In November, the author was advised by the U.S. Army Corps of Engineers, which has jurisdiction over the Youghiogheny River Lake, that the water level would remain higher than the bridge. Plans to return and photograph the old Yough frog were canceled.)

Not far beyond is the site of Fort Necessity and, nearby, the Mount Washington Tavern, once a favorite stopover on the old road and now, meticulously restored, a historic site administered by the National Park Service. Searight catalogued some two hundred taverns along the road in just Maryland and Pennsylvania. Most are gone, but a surprising number remain, even if often disguised as tumble-down relics. Others have reverted to private residences. Tomlinson's, the tavern known to Washington as Tumberson's and perhaps the most famous on the old road, has traded fame for anonymity in its old age. It is still there, but as a very private residence, with kids' swings in the yard and a picnic table in back. There's not even a plaque to tell of its glorious past.

Some of the old taverns, however, are still in business, or lately restored to their original function. The old Mountain

House atop South Mountain in Maryland is now the "Old South Mt. Inn" offering "Food & Drink for All." In Scenery Hill, Pennsylvania, there is the oldest tavern still in use on the road. Once known as Hill's Tavern, it is now the Century Inn, and has been feeding hungry travelers in the same dining room since 1794. It also takes overnight guests in the same second-floor bedrooms that lodged heyday travelers, often two-three-four-five to a bed (sexes in separate rooms). Across the street is a smaller place the Century Inn uses for overflow guests. This one will not be restored to its original use. It is one of the National Road's old bawdyhouses. Laurel Hill still has its Summit House, now Mount Summit Inn. The Red Brick Tavern in Lafayette, Ohio, since its opening in 1837, has served countless guests, including Presidents Adams (J.Q.), Van Buren, Harrison, Tyler, Taylor, and Harding. No overnights anymore, though; the old bedrooms upstairs are for private dining parties. The Archer House in Marshall, Illinois, built in 1841, is that state's oldest hotel, though like the Red Brick it has long since stopped lodging guests. It is open daily for brunch and lunch (salads, croissant sandwiches, and the like) and on Saturday night for dinner. Its presidential register includes Lincoln and Cleveland. None of the existing taverns seems to offer such old-time fare as venison cutlets, grouse, squirrel, or salted bear meat, cold. Or johnnycakes. Or ham and eggs for dinner, as Andrew Jackson ordered on the way to his inauguration. One suspects, however, that if today's president arrived at dinnertime and asked for Andy's favorite, the chef would gladly rustle it up.

It is only a few miles farther until we begin our descent from the steepest of the Alleghenies, a drop of some 1,900 feet to Uniontown. On this Tuesday of our trip, it has been gray and threatening since noon, and sprinkling since midafternoon. Now, in late afternoon, on this steepest of descents westbound, a torrential rain obliterates all of what ought to be a spectacular view and cuts our speed to not much more than 20 miles per hour. Nothing much is visible beyond the windshield wipers, set at high speed. But a return visit on a gloriously beautiful day confirms Uria Brown: "a delightful Prospect indeed; leads the mind in spite of the Heart to contemplate the Promised Land"; or Mary Reed Eastman: "in every direction as far as the eye could reach, [it] surpassed in beauty anything I had ever seen." And indeed, the passing of a hundred and fifty years has not diminished this prospect of Paradise.

Uniontown was among the most important of stops on the old road but little remembers. There's nothing to remind the casual visitor—not even the name of the main street (it's Main Street again). And for a town so prominent in the glorious

years! The town of old Tom Searight! Searight, before his death
in 1899, left instructions that he be buried near the National
Road. In fact, his grave in Oak Grove Cemetery, hard by the old
road, is as close as it could be dug. Only the sidewalk separates
it from the traffic that rumbles by.

Some 5 miles west of Uniontown—shades of Washington's
cabin!—is a talking toll house. Searight's Toll House (1835) has
been preserved as meticulously as the one 6 miles west of
Cumberland but has the added advantage of being able to give
you, at the push of a button, several minutes' worth of history.
The road along here has just been freshly paved. Neither a
cavity nor a precipitous declivity in sight. R. J. Meigs would be
proud.

Brownsville used to be another important stop for travelers, a
reminder of which is the still-standing Brashear House, a leading tavern on the old road from whose door Lafayette addressed
the townspeople in 1825. The memorable event is recorded on
a plaque nearby, but the historicity of the building itself is
transformed by a "Dr. Pepper" sign hanging over the street.
While this advertisement may not be colossal, here is another
tavern "renovated... but with soft drinks." Other than the Brashear,
Brownsville has lost all trace of the road. Yet Matilda Houstoun,
traveling the National Road in the late 1840s and finding
Brownsville a town "dirty with smoke, and coal, and manufactures," might still be able to fancy herself in a Staffordshire
village back home in England.

Near Beallsville is a modern-day phenomenon of the old
road—a statue, heroic in proportions (18 feet high, including
base), of a pioneer woman, a baby in her arms, and a young boy
clutching at her homespun skirts. It is a dynamic piece of
sculpture, as it was meant to be: the "Madonna of the Trail," a
memorial to the pioneer mothers of covered wagon days,
erected by the National Society of the Daughters of the American Revolution in 1928. One finds it an impressive sight—
except that, in driving west another 45 miles or so, one sees
what looks like the same statue in Wheeling, West Virginia. And
indeed it is, exactly the same. And then 180 miles west, exactly
the same statue in Springfield, Ohio; and then 65 miles west,
exactly the same statue in Richmond, Indiana; and then Vandalia,
Illinois.

There is something bizarre about continually being confronted
with what one first thought was unique. Statues don't travel, and
certainly not when they're 17 tons. Yet this one seems to be
following you cross-country, somehow always beating you around
the next bend and, without any hint of being breathless for
running the faster race, is suddenly standing there, as if that is

The Madonna of the Trail, Vandalia, Illinois.

where the sculptor shaped it with hammer and chisel, uniquely and for all time. How there can be so many alike is explainable: the Madonnas of the Trail weren't shaped with hammer and chisel; each was cast of a mineral substance called algonite.

Into what is now a part of Wheeling and was then Elm Grove, we make a hard right turn over Little Wheeling Creek. The bridge has the appearance of many a bridge built in the 1920s and 1930s—concrete deck and poured concrete balustrade along the side. There's little to distinguish it except a big hump in the middle. Twentieth-century bridges are relatively flat. This bridge that daily absorbs the rumble of urban traffic, eighteen-wheelers and all, is one of the original National Road bridges. Unlike others seen so far, this one's not part of a park or otherwise lying disused, off to the side of a new alignment of U.S. 40. This one is still on duty. Given its now urban location, its alignment still makes sense; and though built in 1817, its construction is formidable enough for urban traffic and its width sufficient for three tractor-trailer trucks side by side.

From down below, we can see the familiar outline of a National Road bridge, its hump owing to its arched structure, and some of the uncoursed limestone of which it was constructed. Otherwise, a peeling concrete veneer applied to the bridge in 1958 successfully (save its hump) disguises its origin, and one suspects that few of those traversing it daily realize they are adequately supported by a stone-and-mortar structure 170 years old.

Just over the Ohio River, in Brookside, we find the first sign of evolution beyond the original terminus of Wheeling—a new kind of milepost, unique to Ohio, this particular one inscribed "Cumberland 135." Evolutionary, too, is the countryside; it's beginning to look a little more midwestern now—flatter and more open. Long gone are the awesome Alleghenies. Gone, too, for the most part, are the relatively more abundant traces of the old road that could be found in the Alleghenies—though not entirely gone. East and west of New Concord, Ohio, are two of the S-bridges that are a curiosity of the National Road and a product of the pragmatism it typified. Where the road crossed a stream obliquely, the early engineers found it more difficult and expensive to construct a bridge than where the road crossed perpendicularly; so they made the crossing perpendicular and curved the bridge obliquely around and back in the shape of an S. The S-bridge to the west of New Concord, unlike other decommissioned bridges along the way, is accessible by car. Now we can say we have actually driven on part of the *old* National Road. The bridge won't take us anywhere, of course, except the other end. There is a marker of the Ohio Historical

Society nearby noting that, prior to our crossing, "Coaches, Conestoga wagons, herds of livestock, pioneers on foot or horseback, peddlers, soldiers, beggars—these and many others have crossed this bridge on the National Road since 1830."

There is a unique reminder of the old road in Norwich, Ohio, about halfway between Cambridge and Zanesville—the National Road/Zane Grey Museum (Grey, the writer of western novels, was a native of Zanesville, a town settled by his great-grandfather and an important stop on the old road). The museum was established by the Ohio Historical Society in 1973. Among its exhibits are a diorama showing the development of the road in miniature; displays of historic vehicles, including a Conestoga wagon; and life-size reconstructions of such typical National Road scenes as a tavern common room and a wheelwright's shop.

Near Zanesville is a general store (complete with potbellied stove) that is *not* from the old days. Called Grandma's, and opened only a year ago, it is a reminder that the old road is still alive as a highway of commerce. "You'd be surprised," Grandma Downing tells us, "how many people get off the Interstate and take old 40. I had no idea until the store opened. People like to visit the shops."

On toward the state capital of Columbus. The approach (East Main Street now) is an unending clutter of signs for every known fast-food emporium and gas station—that lone, blinking neon "EATS" sign that lured Thompson Derby to supper now multiplied to profusion. The fact that the road, by design, was made as straight as possible only adds to the sense of clutter; there's not even a bend for relief. Downtown Columbus, however, is pleasant enough, the road passing directly by the statehouse and a mall lined with the flags of all the states.

West of Columbus we're in the flattest country so far. The sky is a crisp, Midwestern blue heaped with marshmallow clouds; the road as straight as Congress meant it to be. Milepost 17—the Ohio kind—is the first sign of the old road since the museum.

Richmond, Indiana, just over the Ohio line, still has a gate at the side of the road that William Hale might have swung on; and Linden Hill, down which Grandmother Harlan swooped in her vibrating monster, is still part of the topography of the old road, which in this part of town is framed by many of the same, sturdy old homes that were there that memorable night in 1911. Otherwise, there seem to be so few reminders of the old road that the "National Rd. Auto Body" and the "National Drive-In Theater" stand out for their relative importance. But the road has not been forgotten. We discover, for example, that

Near Grantsville, Maryland, May 1989, the National Pike Festival: wagon trains and garb of pioneer days. The annual festival covers a 200-mile route through six counties in Pennsylvania and Maryland.

Courtesy of the *Maryland Cracker Barrel*

Richmond's daily *Palladium-Item* has just run a whole series of articles, thirty-six in all, about the National Road in Indiana, and the people and places along the road today. The writer is Dick Reynolds, the *Palladium-Item*'s retired managing editor, who grew up along the National Road during the Great Depression. His most vivid memory is of Indy 500 weekends, when kids, most of them too poor to go to the race, let alone travel out of state, sat by the side of the National Road watching a seemingly endless stream of cars—exotic motorcars like Stutzes, Packards, Auburns, Cords, with license plates from exotic, faraway places like New York, Connecticut, and Massachusetts—passing through Richmond "like foreigners" on their way to the famous race in Indianapolis, and a day or two later coming back through Richmond on their way home. "People had picnics on their lawns, so they could watch. For the kids, many of whom had never been out of Indiana, it was the greatest thing in the world."

In Lewisville, a few miles west, there is a picturesquely dilapidated structure that could have had no purpose earlier in time other than to await the periodic screech of stagecoach wheels; today it sits forlornly in the silence of a different era. Greenfield has its James Whitcomb Riley home (open to visitors), with its "upper-story looking squarely down upon the main street, the main highway from East to West, historic in its day." And indeed, from the second story, one can peer through a lace-curtained window and, across U.S. 40, see a street sign on the corner that says "W. Main St."

Terre Haute: To the Bestes, it was a "village in the Far West"; and while it is only in the far west of Indiana, to these weary travelers of 1851 it may well have seemed that an entire continent had been crossed in reaching it. Here it was that this brave family endured its siege of illness, and here that they laid to rest their darling Isabel. From Lucy's account of the funeral, it is possible to locate the likely cemetery in which the child was buried—a small Roman Catholic cemetery roughly 2 miles from the center of town. Let us see if we are right.

It is a suitably gloomy morning, a rain of the night before leaving the grass soggy. For nearly two hours, our shoes dampening, we pace among the tombstones, some of them recent, others from the late nineteenth and early twentieth centuries. At last—a gravestone from the 1850s, and another, and indeed a whole cluster from the mid-nineteenth century. Perhaps, after all . . . One by one, we examine them until all have been checked. Alas, there is none with Isabel's name, but there are many with no name at all. A hundred and fifty years of pelting rains and melting hoarfrosts have obliterated many of the inscriptions.

The potbelly stove, inevitable mainstay of the general store. Above:
R. H. Wilson & Son's, Clear Spring, Maryland.

Yet it is surely one of these now nameless and yearless memorials that marks the place where a little traveler ended her journey.

Illinois, of all the states, has the fewest reminders of the old road, which is explainable. The National Road had the least impact here. By the time it reached Vandalia, the railroad had crossed the Mississippi.

At last, on to Vandalia, an unpretentious but likable little town. Long since replaced as the state capital, it would no longer disappoint Edmund Flagg, whose notion of what the First City of a state ought to look like was a bit more grandiose than Vandalia's idea of it. At the corner of the square is a small plaque, about a foot or so high: "Cumberland Road. Vandalia was the western terminus of the Cumberland or National Road which extended eighty feet wide for 591 miles from Cumberland, Maryland through Pennsylvania, Ohio, Indiana."

So we're there—the end of the most historic single road in America—although *our* trip, all the way from Baltimore, has been more like 750 miles. With all of our taking of notes and photographs, it has been ten days, an average of 75 miles a day. Given an eight-hour day of travel, that's roughly 9 miles per hour—barely better than the "five to six miles an hour" William Blane recorded for a stagecoach traveling the National Road in 1822. Whizzing along Interstate 70 the whole distance, we could easily have made the whole trip in less than two days.

But look what we would have missed along the way.

The National Pike, Sideling Hill, Maryland.

Tips for Travelers

For those who are interested in driving the route of the old road, it generally follows U.S. Route 40 or 40 Alt. As a rule, where there is an alternate route, that is more likely to be the old road, the main route being the more modern highway, though not necessarily. In some places, the old road has been superseded by Interstate 70 so that there is not a trace of it. Yet for the most part, I-70, which generally parallels the route of the old National Road, has had a salutary impact by diverting much of the traffic, especially the trucks, permitting a more relaxing drive over the old route. Indeed, cutting one's pace from the frenetic speed of Interstate travel and stopping and looking about on one's drive along U.S. 40 or 40 Alt., one can still find relics of the old road, notably some of its noble, stone-arch bridges.

U.S. Geological Survey and local maps will help make it easier to find the old route, for indeed it is still known as "National Road" or "National Pike" or "National Avenue" in many places. The most detailed accounts of the route generally available may be found in the tour sections of the American Guide Series of books for the respective states. Although originally published in the late 1930s and early 1940s, many of these have been reprinted, and they are available in many libraries. While clearly out of date as to modern superhighways, these guides are still for the most part applicable to tours along the old National Road.

Biographical Notes and Sources

The first-person accounts recorded here have generally been condensed to their most relevant and interesting portions. One or two are so brief that they are included in their entirety; in other cases the original journals are so voluminous that the condensation has necessarily been considerable; in all cases the abridging has been done as carefully as possible to preserve context and the integrity of the writer's flow of thought, yet without the usual ellipses that would be distracting in a book meant for reading rather than research. For like reason, *sic* has not been used. Spelling, except for obvious typographical errors in the original, has been preserved as found. This includes place names. For example: there are a number of variations of "Allegheny," all left as found in the original. But it should be remembered that while "Allegheny" may generally be thought of as correct, it is only correct when referring to the mountains, the river, and the county in Pennsylvania; equally correct are "Allegany" (counties in Maryland and New York) and "Alleghany" (counties in North Carolina and Virginia). Individual travelers have additional spellings all their own.

The narratives selected here represent the bulk of such journals known to exist. There are a few other accounts not included because the relevant portions were too brief or because they duplicated other accounts being used that were far more interesting. As a whole, these journals are remarkably informative, not only as to the National Road but as to the life and times that shaped it; many are thoroughly absorbing simply as accounts of human experience.

GEORGE WASHINGTON, (1753–54)

The Journal of George Washington (Williamsburg, 1754), pp. 26–28.

The expedition of 1753–54 was the first of seven journeys Washington made to the Ohio Valley during his lifetime.

A SEAMAN

Archer Butler Hulbert, *Historic Highways of America* (Cleveland, 1902–5), vol. 4, pp. 90–97.

The identity of the seaman is unknown, although he was almost certainly an officer; a mere sailor would not have kept a journal, let alone one so detailed. The contingent of thirty seamen was on loan to General Braddock from Commodore Augustus Keppel, commander of the North American Station of the British Navy, based in Hampton Roads, Virginia.

ROBERT ORME

"Captain Orme's Journal," Historical Society of Pennsylvania, *Memoirs*, vol. 5 (1855), pp. 326–43.

An officer in the Coldstream Guards, which he joined in 1745, Robert Orme was on leave to accompany General Braddock on his expedition to Fort Duquesne. Orme returned to England after Braddock's defeat and in 1756 resigned his commission and retired to private life. About the same time, after an apparently brief courtship, he married Audrey Townshend, daughter of Charles, 3rd Viscount Townshend, to the displeasure of the family, owing to Orme's lesser station. This made Orme the brother-in-law of the Townshend of the Townshend Acts of 1767.

GEORGE WASHINGTON (1784)

Archer Butler Hulbert, ed., *Washington and the West* (New York, 1905), pp. 40–42.

Having resigned his commission, Washington returned home from the Revolutionary War late in 1783, reaching Mount Vernon on Christmas Eve—"a wearied traveler [who had trod] many a painful step with a heavy burden" (letter to a friend early in 1784). Months later, the weariness abated, he was ready for another major travel—his 1784 journey to the Ohio Valley—spurred on in large part by his determination to see a major road opened up to the west.

ROBERT WELLFORD

"Diary of Dr. Robert Wellford," *William and Mary Quarterly*, vol. 11, July 1902, pp. 6–14.

Dr. Robert Wellford (1753–1823) was a native of England who came to America as a surgeon with the First Battalion of Grenadiers late in

1775. He defected from the British Army in Philadelphia in 1778 when it became apparent that his views on humane treatment of American prisoners were sharply at variance with those of his superiors. Among the American prisoners he befriended was Colonel John Spotswood, grandson of Governor Spotswood of Virginia. At Spotswood's behest, Wellford settled in Virginia after the war and made his home in Fredericksburg. He married in 1781 and continued practicing medicine until his death in 1823.

ELIE WILLIAMS

"Journal kept by Elie Williams during examination of route for Cumberland Road by the Commissioners in 1806." Ms., National Archives, Record Group 77, Entry #179, Box 5.

Certainly one of the prime shapers of the National Road, Elie Williams (1750–1822) was a native of Prince Georges County, Maryland, near what is now the District of Columbia, but he spent much of his life in Washington County (Hagerstown), through which passed the National Road. Although his first name is commonly found as "Eli," he used "Elie" (pronounced "Ee-lee") in his handwritten journal, and this is the correct form. Williams was a colonel in the Revolutionary War, serving under his brother, General Otho Williams. In 1794 he was commissary under General Light-Horse Harry Lee at the Whiskey Rebellion. He was the first clerk of the court of Washington County, later also serving as a judge of the Orphans Court. In 1797, he was a member, along with Charles Carroll and others, of a planning committee for the Baltimore Turnpike. Following his 1806 appointment as a Cumberland Road commissioner by Jefferson, Congress in 1807 appointed him surveyor for the proposed Chesapeake and Ohio Canal (on which actual construction did not begin until 1828). He was elected to the Maryland House of Delegates in 1822 but died before taking office—ironically, in light of his responsibilities in laying out the Cumberland Road, "of a disease contracted whilst surveying the route of the proposed [C&O] Canal," according to an early biography.

URIA BROWN

"Uria Brown's Journal," *Maryland Historical Magazine,* vol. 10 (1915), pp. 275–83.

Uria Brown was born in Chester County, Pennsylvania, in 1769, the great-grandson of a William Brown who migrated to America from England in 1682. Uria learned blacksmithing from his father, David, and at first practiced that trade. Along the way he managed to study surveying and conveyancing, and he eventually made that his profession, maintaining an office in Baltimore. He was also the first teacher at McKim's Free School, founded in Baltimore in 1821, a position he held until 1827. He married in 1793 and had four daughters.

ADLARD WELBY

Adlard Welby, *A Visit to North America* (London, 1821); in Reuben Gold Thwaites, ed., *Early Western Travels, 1748–1846* (Cleveland, 1905), vol. 12, pp. 200–205, 278–90.

All that is known of Adlard Welby is that he was an Englishman of some affluence. He traveled in America with a valet, in his own carriage, and had little patience with the seeming rusticity of American life. His diary has frequent complaints about the roads, the food, the accommodations, and the crudity of American manners.

JAMES HALL

James Hall, *Letters from the West* (London, 1828), pp. 54–57.

James Hall, a jurist and author, was born in Philadelphia in 1793, the son of the U.S. marshal for the district of Pennsylvania and grandson of the Reverend John Ewing, provost of the University of Pennsylvania. During the War of 1812, he served as a lieutenant in a regiment commanded by Winfield Scott. He subsequently studied law, was admitted to the bar, and moved to Illinois, where he became a circuit judge and then state treasurer, making his office in Vandalia. He was a prolific writer and founded the *Illinois Weekly Intelligencer* and the *Illinois Monthly Magazine.* In 1833, he moved to Cincinnati and continued his career as a writer and editor there until his death, in 1868.

WILLIAM BLANE

[William Newnham Blane], *An Excursion Through the United States and Canada* (London, 1824), pp. 86–91.

William Newnham Blane, a self-described "English gentleman," was twenty-two when he began his two-year journey through the United States and Canada. Two years after completing his trip, he died, at the age of twenty-five.

R. J. MEIGS, JR.

"Letter from the Postmaster General in Relation to the State and Condition of the Cumberland Road," *U.S. House Documents,* 17th Congress, 2nd Session, vol. 1 (Washington, 1823).

Born in Middletown, Connecticut, in 1764, Return Jonathan Meigs, Jr., graduated from Yale in 1785 and soon after was admitted to the Connecticut bar. In 1788, he was married to Sophia Wright and moved to Marietta, Ohio, where, in 1798, he was appointed a territorial judge. He was a strong supporter of statehood, and was named Ohio's first chief justice when it became a state. From 1808 to 1810, he served as U.S. senator, and then was elected governor of Ohio, holding that post until 1814, when he resigned to become Madison's postmaster-general. He continued in office until 1823—the year after his National Road trip—when he resigned because of ill health. He died a year later. During his tenure as postmaster-general, the number of post offices increased from 3,000 to 5,200, while the mileage of post roads more than doubled, from 41,000 to 85,000.

CHARLES FENNO HOFFMAN

[Charles Fenno Hoffman], *A Winter in the West* (New York, 1835), vol. 1, pp. 47–54.

Of the many first-person narratives appearing in this book, only that of Charles Fenno Hoffman (1806–1884) is known to have been written to defray the expenses of his travels. His narrative, in installments, was first published as a paid contribution to the *New York American* (1833–34) and subsequently became the two-volume book cited above. Over and above that, Hoffman is to be appreciated by later-day writers for his acquiescence to reality in temporarily setting aside his writing career in 1841 to accept the relatively pecunious post of third chief clerk in the office of the surveyor of customs of the Port of New York at a relatively munificent $1,000 a year. Within three years he had parlayed that into the deputy surveyorship at some undisclosed increase in salary, only to return to writing full-time through the vicissitudes of the political patronage system. As a writer of both poetry and prose, he became an acquaintance of Edgar Allan Poe. For a time, in 1840, he was also associate editor, with Horace Greeley, of the *New-Yorker* (no connection to the present magazine). In 1849, after a year of treatment by a specialist in mental disorders, he was admitted to a state hospital in Harrisburg, Pennsylvania, and continued there the remaining thirty-four years of his life. The extent of his travels over the National Road and throughout the Midwest by horseback from October 1833 through June 1834 is the more remarkable in light of the fact that his right leg was so crushed in an accident at the age of eleven that it had to be amputated.

THOMAS B. SEARIGHT

Thomas B. Searight, *The Old Pike* (Uniontown, Pa., 1894), pp. 16–18.

Thomas Brownfield Searight made a vocation of the law and an avocation of the National Road. Born on the road in Menallen Township, Fayette County, Pennsylvania, in 1827, he graduated in 1848 from Washington and Jefferson College, where James G. Blaine was a close friend as well as schoolmate. Besides practicing law in Fayette County throughout his life, Searight served in both the State Senate and House of Representatives as well as several terms as chief clerk of the courts in Fayette County. He was a delegate to the Democratic national conventions that nominated George B. McClellan (1864) and Grover Cleveland (1884). In 1857, he married Rose Flenniken, daughter of the U.S. Minister to Denmark under President Polk. As a historian of the National Road, he collected reminiscences and other memorabilia over a number of years. After his death in 1899, he was buried, at his request, in sight of the road.

WILLIAM H. WILLS

"A Southern Traveler's Diary in 1840," Southern History Association, *Publications,* vol. 7, no. 6 (November 1903), pp. 427–31.

A native of Tarboro, North Carolina, William Henry Wills (1809–89), as a young man, received informal business training from a kinsman, Spencer D. Cotten. But he joined the Methodist Church at the age of twenty-one and received his license to preach a year later. He then devoted himself primarily to the church, serving as an itinerant preacher for the North Carolina Conference of the Methodist Protestant Church for most of his life. After Cotten's death in 1837, he set aside his preaching duties for several years to act as administrator of his kinsman's estate, settlement of which required a visit to Mississippi and Alabama in 1840, the trip that took him over the National Road. He was married in 1835 to Anna Maria Baker of Halifax County and had nine children. In 1866, he was presiding officer of the national conference of the Methodist Protestant Church. Stricken with paralysis in 1884, he remained bedridden until his death in 1889.

JOHN DEETS

Searight, *The Old Pike,* pp. 120–22.

John Deets, wagon driver and seemingly the personification of obscurity, probably never saw his name in print. Could he have known a century and a half ago that not only his name but his account of travels on the National Road would appear in a book, nearly side by side with the writings of the Father of His Country, he would probably have succumbed to a moment of astonishment and then, unfazed, hitched his team to his wagon and trekked off serenely down the road. We know from Searight that he was a wagoner as early as 1826; that he had a brother, Michael, four years older, who started wagoning the National Road in 1822; that he was born (or at least spent his early years) in Menallen Township, Fayette County, Pennsylvania; that he moved to Guernsey County, Ohio, in 1835; and that he was still living in 1893.

JESSE J. PIERSOL

Searight, *The Old Pike,* pp. 142–43.

Much the same can be said of Jesse Piersol as of Deets, with these particulars: son of a wagoner; started wagoning himself on the National Road at least by the early 1840s; later turned to farming and became prosperous at it, maintaining a farm in Franklin Township, Fayette County, Pennsylvania; was not only alive in 1893 but "of vigorous health and unimpaired memory" (Searight).

WILLIAM FAUX

William Faux, *Memorable Days in America* (London, 1823), pp. 163–73.

Nothing is known of William Faux except that he was a gentleman farmer from Somersham, England, and like other of his countrymen, kept a journal of his travels that he published on his return. Unfortunately for him (and others) this was a time when the British press was relishing such accounts as a means of disparaging American life and institutions. Faux's descriptiveness played into their hands. A review of *Memorable Days* in *Blackwoods Magazine,* November 1823, put him down as "a simpleton of the first water, a capital specimen of a village John Bull, for the first time roaming far away from his native valley— staring at everything, and grumbling at most."

WILLIAM OWEN

"The Diary of William Owen," Indiana Historical Society, *Publications,* vol. 4 (1906), pp. 47–50.

William Owen (1802–42) was the second son of social reformer Robert Owen (1771–1858) and brother of Robert Dale Owen (1801–77), also a reformer and later a member of Congress for Indiana. William was alone among the sons to accompany Robert Owen on his 1824 journey to establish his ill-fated social community at New Harmony, Indiana. He remained after his father's return in 1825, managing family business interests, serving as a director of the Evansville branch of the State Bank of Indiana, and editing the *New Harmony Gazette,* which the family had established. He also organized a county agricultural society. He died in New Harmony at the age of forty.

MARY REED EASTMAN

"The Diaries of Mary Reed Eastman," vol. 2, pp. 56–65. Ms., Schlesinger Library, Radcliffe College.

Born in Marblehead, Massachusetts, in 1806, Mary Reed was a descendant of John Howland, a *Mayflower* passenger, and granddaughter of Captain William Blackler, who captained the boat that took George Washington across the Delaware River on Christmas night, 1776. She had a brother and two sisters. Little is known of her early years, though from the quality of her diaries it would appear she was well educated. In 1832, she married Ornan Eastman (1796–1874), a native of Amherst, Massachusetts, and a graduate of Yale who studied theology at Andover Seminary and then began a lifelong association with the American Tract Society, based in New York City. Through this affiliation he traveled widely, including, as general agent for the Mississippi Valley, the travels described in Mary's journal. The Eastmans had three sons and three daughters. Mary died in 1878.

EDMUND FLAGG

[Edmund Flagg], *The Far West: or a Tour Beyond the Mountains* (New York, 1838); in *Early Western Travels,* vol. 26, pp. 243–44, 359–60.

Born in Wescasset, Maine, November 24, 1815, Flagg attended Bowdoin College, graduating in 1835, the same year he moved to Louisville, Kentucky, with his mother and sister. He was associated with the Louisville *Journal* as editorial writer and correspondent for many years. He also served at one time as secretary to the U.S. minister to Berlin; as U.S. consul in Venice; and as librarian of copyrights in the Department of the Interior. The journal of his western travels originally appeared in installments in the Louisville *Journal* as "Sketches of a Traveller." They were subsequently published in two volumes by Harper and Brothers in New York. He died in 1890.

J. RICHARD BESTE

J. Richard Beste, *The Wabash: or Adventures of an English Gentleman's Family in the Interior of America* (London, 1855), vol. 1, pp. 259–60, 275–76, 290–99, 311–12; vol. 2, pp. 1–38, 175–77; 187–89.

John Richard Digby Beste (1806–85), an English gentleman "in the rank of country gentry," visited America with a large family of children (six girls and five boys), as he tells us in the prologue to *The Wabash.* Beyond that there is only this scant information: "Like the Swiss family Robinson Crusoes [sic], we stand before the reader—mysteriously driven forth to wander and to live, for a few months, in a character as new to ourselves as our real position is unsuspected by those amongst whom we travel [the inhabitants of the Backwoods]." It is the more regrettable we know so little about Beste, for his narrative is surely one of the most poignantly written and amply detailed of all accounts of travels on the National Road. As he wished, he travels incognito.

MATILDA HOUSTOUN

Mrs. [Matilda Charlotte (Jesse) Fraser] Houstoun, *Hesperos: or Travels in the West* (London, 1850), pp. 239–63.

Matilda Houstoun (1815[?]–92) was about thirty-two and had been married for several years at the time of her National Road travels (she was already "Mrs. Houstoun" when an earlier book was published in 1844). She later wrote several novels and other works. Save one fragmentary date, the travels recorded in *Hesperos* are undated as to year. But there are clues firmly establishing that it was in 1847 that she traveled the National Road. For one, there is her observation that George Washington's defeat at Fort Necessity (1754) was "ninety-three years ago." Corroborating clues are "Monday the 4th of October" as the date of a severe storm at sea during her voyage from England and her recollection of visiting in Washington and getting to meet President Polk. Polk was president from 1845 to 1849, and the only year within that period that October 4 fell on a Monday was 1847.

JOHN LEWIS PEYTON

John Lewis Peyton, *Over the Alleghanies* (London, 1870), pp. 20–28.

Virginia-born John Lewis Peyton (1824–96), after briefly attending Virginia Military Institute, received a law degree from the University of Virginia in 1844 and practiced in Staunton until the Fillmore administration in 1852 sent him on a secret mission to England, France, and Austria. He then lived briefly in Illinois but returned to Virginia in 1856. A Whig, he opposed secession; but once it came, he helped organize a regiment of the Confederate Army. He himself, however, spent the war years and those afterward as agent of the state of North Carolina in Europe, and it was while there that he published his recollections of his trip over the Alleghenies. He returned to Virginia and authored several other books.

WILLIAM HENRY RIDEING

[William Henry Rideing], "The Old National Pike," *Harper's,* November 1879.

William Henry Rideing, born in Liverpool, England, in 1853, might have followed his father (an early official of the Cunard Line) and great-uncle (a rear admiral in the Royal Navy) to a career at sea. Instead, at age sixteen, with both parents dead, he came to America and embarked on a career as a journalist—at first with the *Springfield* [Massachusetts] *Republican* and then with the *New York Tribune* and then as a "handy man of literature" (his phrase for a freelancer), contributing prolifically to various magazines. At one time he was also a special correspondent for the *New York Times* covering exploration of the Southwest. He was the author of a number of books. Rideing died in 1918 in Brookline, Massachusetts.

* * *

The illustrations accompanying Rideing's article were the work of a twenty-six-year-old artist later to become famous both as an illustrator and an author of books of adventure—Howard Pyle (1853–1911). It was only the year before that an illustration of his first appeared in *Harper's.* As an author, beginning with *The Merry Adventures of Robin Hood,* in 1883, Pyle had great popularity with generations of young readers. Among his students was artist N. C. Wyeth.

JAMES WHITCOMB RILEY

James Whitcomb Riley, *A Child-World* (Indianapolis, 1896), pp. 17–19.

Too nostalgic and sentimental for post–World War I America, James Whitcomb Riley is more often than not forgotten today; in his time, he was among the best-known and most widely read poets in America. His affection for the National Road—on which he was born, in Greenfield, Indiana, in 1849 and on which he died in Indianapolis in 1916—was second to none among its chroniclers.

RUFUS ROCKWELL WILSON

Rufus Rockwell Wilson, "The National Pike and Its Memories," *New England Magazine*, May 1902, pp. 306, 317–20.

Rufus Rockwell Wilson (1865–1949) was best known in his time as an expert on Lincoln, about whom he wrote more than twenty books, including *The Uncollected Works of Abraham Lincoln*. He was a native of Troy, Pennsylvania, and wrote for newspapers in a number of Pennsylvania towns, including Washington, on the National Road, as well as the Brooklyn *Eagle*. He was also at one time secretary of the National Association of Cotton Manufacturers. In his later years he was president of the Primavera Press and the Wilson Book Company, his own publishing firms.

ARCHER BUTLER HULBERT

Archer Butler Hulbert, *Historic Highways of America*, vol. 10, pp. 174–80, 186–87.

As a professor of American history, Archer Butler Hulbert clearly had a fondness for the historical importance of roads, writing a number of books and articles. From 1905 to 1914, he was a lecturer for the U.S. Office of Public Roads, and later he was chairman of the historic highways committee of the National Highways Association. Born in Bennington, Vermont, in 1873, he received a B.A., an honorary M.A., and a doctorate degree from Marietta College, teaching there also from 1904 to 1918, and then for two years at Clark University. In 1920, he joined the faculty of Colorado College and remained there until his death in 1933.

WILLIAM BAYARD HALE

William Bayard Hale, "The Old National Road," *Century Magazine*, December 1911.

William Bayard Hale was born in Richmond, Indiana, in 1869 and started his career as an Episcopal clergyman (rector of the Church of Our Savior, Middleboro, Massachusetts). After 1900, he switched to journalism, at one time or another being associated with the *New York Times Sunday Magazine*, *Philadelphia Public Ledger*, and *New York American*, with the last as chief Central European correspondent in 1917. He was a friend of President Wilson, who, in 1913, sent Hale as a confidential envoy to the Carranza Government in Mexico; later Hale broke with Wilson, bitterly attacking him in a book. He died in 1924.

ALBERT DOUGLAS

Albert Douglas, "Auto Trip Over the Old National Road," Ohio State Archaeological and Historical Society, *Publications*, vol. 18 (1909), pp. 504–12.

Albert Douglas was a member of the U.S. House of Representatives for Ohio's 11th Congressional District from 1907 to 1911. In 1921, he was named by President Harding as special ambassador to represent the United States at Peru's centenary of independence. A native of Chillicothe, Ohio, he graduated from Kenyon College and Harvard Law School. From 1876 to 1880, he served as prosecuting attorney for Ross County, Ohio. A candidate for governor in 1899, but withdrew prior to the Republican nominating convention. He was a trustee of both Kenyon College and Ohio University. After many years as an invalid, he died in 1935, at the age of eighty-two.

ROBERT BRUCE

Robert Bruce, "The Status of the Old National Road," *Motor* magazine, March 1913.

Robert Bruce, who was born in 1873, was the author of several historical books as well as a number of magazine articles advocating good roads. He lived for a time in Clinton, New York.

PHILIP JORDAN

Philip Jordan, *The National Road* (Indianapolis: Bobbs-Merrill Company, 1948), excerpts from Chapter 23, "U.S. 40."

Philip Dillon Jordan, the author of a number of books and many articles on American history, taught at Long Island University and Miami University of Ohio before becoming professor of history at the University of Minnesota, a position he held from 1946 until his retirement in 1969. He was born in 1904 in Burlington, Iowa, where at age sixteen he organized the Boy Scout movement after attending the World Boy Scout Jubilee in London and reporting on it for the Burlington *Hawk-Eye*. A graduate of Northwestern University (B.S. and M.S. degrees), he received a doctorate in history from the University of Iowa. He was married to the former Marion Valentine, and had one daughter, Martha. He was a member of many historical and professional societies, a fellow of the Royal Historical Society in England, a consultant to the National Archives and Records Service, a curator of the State Historical Society of Iowa, and an honorary member of the Hiawatha Indian Tribe in Minnesota. He died in 1980 in Burlington, where he had lived since his retirement.

MERRITT IERLEY

The author's narrative is a composite of notes made during trips along the National Road in 1988 and 1989.

Merritt Ierley, who makes his home in Sussex, New Jersey, is an alumnus of Gill/St. Bernard's School, Gladstone, New Jersey, and the

College of William and Mary. He is a former journalist, and was at one time an editor at the *Virginia Gazette*. His first book, *The Year That Tried Men's Souls*, appeared in 1976. A journalistic reconstruction of the world of 1776, with an introduction by the former director of the American Press Institute, it was published in both the United States and England. He is also the author of *With Charity for All: Welfare and Society, Ancient Times to the Present*. Ierley is also a composer, primarily of choral music. His works have been performed around the country, among other places at the New York Cultural Center, the College of William and Mary, and the Memorial Arts Center in Atlanta.

Additional Sources

Margaret W. Anderson, "Biographical Notes on Mary Reed Eastman," *Muskingum Annals: Number Four* (Zanesville: Muskingum Valley Archaeological Survey, 1987).

Seymour Dunbar, *A History of Travel in America* (Indianapolis: Bobbs-Merrill, 1915).

Maurice O. Eldridge, "Progress of Road Building in the United States," *L.A.W. Magazine* [League of American Wheelman], n.s. vol. 1, no. 5, (October 1900).

Earle R. Forrest, *History of the National Pike in Fayette and Somerset Counties* (Ms., National Park Service, Fort Necessity National Battlefield, Farmington, Pennsylvania).

John Kennedy Lacock, "Braddock Road," *Pennsylvania Magazine of History and Biography,* vol. 38 (1914), no. 1.

Carroll Miller (Mrs.), "The Romance of the National Pike," *Western Pennsylvania Historical Magazine,* vol. 10, no. 1 (January 1927).

John B. Rae, *The Road and the Car in American Life* (Cambridge: M.I.T. Press, 1971).

John Robinson, *Highways and Our Environment* (New York: McGraw-Hill, 1971).

Albert C. Rose, "The National Pike or Cumberland Road," *Road Builders News,* April 1938.

Norris F. Schneider, *The National Road: Main Street of America* (Columbus: Ohio Historical Society, 1975).

G. L. Waddell, "National Old Trails Road," *National Republic,* December 1930.